ARMENIAN APOSTOLIC CHRISTIANS

Books LLC®, Reference Series, Memphis, USA, 2011. ISBN: 9781156023327. www.booksllc.net. Copyright: http://creativecommons.org/licenses/by-sa/3.0/deed.en

Table of Contents

Armenian Apostolic Christians
- Hasmik Papian 1
- Komitas Vardapet 2
- Robert Kocharyan 4
- Serzh Sargsyan 5
- Tiridates III of Armenia 6

Bishops of the Armenian Apostolic Church
- Husik Santurjan 8
- Sebouh Chouldjian 8

Catholicoi of Armenia
- Abraham III of Armenia 9
- Ananias I of Armenia 10
- Asdvadzadur of Armenia 10
- Aspuraces I 10
- Bartholomew the Apostle 11
- Basil of Ani 11
- Catholicos of All Armenians 11
- Christopher II of Armenia 11
- Daniel I of Armenia 12
- David I of Armenia 12
- Dertad I 12
- Garabed II of Armenia 12
- George II of Armenia 13
- George VI of Armenia 13
- Gomidas 14
- Gregory II the Martyrophile 14
- Gregory the Illuminator 15
- Hovhannes Draskhanakerttsi 16
- Isaac of Armenia 17
- Jude the Apostle 18
- Karekin I 20
- Karekin II 21
- Khachig I of Armenia 22
- Khoren I 22
- Khoren I of Armenia 22
- Lazar I of Armenia 22
- List of Catholicoi of Armenia 23
- Mashdotz I 25
- Mkrtich Khrimian 25
- Moses III of Armenia 26
- Nahabed I of Armenia 26
- Nerses III the Builder 27
- Nerses V 27
- Parsegh of Cilicia 27
- Peter I of Armenia 28
- Pharen I of Armenia 28
- Sahak I 28
- Sahak III 28
- Sarkis II the Relic-Carrier 29
- Sarkis I of Armenia 29
- Seats of the Catholicos of Armenians 29
- St. Aristaces I 29
- St. Husik 29
- St. Husik I 29
- St. Nerses I 30
- St. Vrtanes I 30
- Vazgen I 30
- Yeghishe I 31
- Zacharias I of Armenia 31
- Zaven I 31

Introduction

Purchase of this book entitles you to a free trial membership in the publisher's book club at www.booksllc.net. (Time limited offer.) Simply enter the barcode number from the back cover onto the membership form. The book club entitles you to select from hundreds of thousands of books at no additional charge. You can also download a digital copy of this and related books to read on the go. Simply enter the title or subject onto the search form to find them.

Each chapter in this book ends with a URL to a hyperlinked online version. Type the URL exactly as it appears. If you change the URL's capitalization it won't work. Use the online version to access related pages, websites, footnotes, tables, color photos, updates. Click the version history tab to see the chapter's contributors. Click the edit link to suggest changes.

A large and diverse editor base collaboratively wrote the book, not a single author. After a long process of discussion and debate, the chapters gradually took on a neutral point of view reached through consensus. Additional editors expanded and contributed to chapters striving to achieve balance and comprehensive coverage. This reduced the regional or cultural bias found in many other books and provided access and breadth on subject matter otherwise little documented.

Hasmik Papian

Hasmik Papian (Armenian: Հասմիկ Պապյան; born 1961 in Yerevan) is an Armenian soprano.

Biography

Hasmik Papian graduated from High Academy in Yerevan first as a violinist, then as a singer. After her debut at the Armenian National Opera, she was invited as a soloist among others by Opera Bonn and Deutsche Oper am Rhein, Düsseldorf, Germany. Soon, she started an international career and has since appeared at numerous theaters, including the most prestigious operatic stages and concert houses in the world like The Metropolitan Opera and Carnegie Hall New York, San Francisco Opera, Washington National Opera, La Scala of Milan, Opéra Bastille in Paris, Gran Theatre del Liceu Barcelona, Teatro Real Madrid, London Wigmore Hall, the Vienna State Opera and Musikverein Vienna, Concertgebouw and De Nederlandse Opera Amsterdam, Zurich Opera, Mariinsky Theatre St. Petersburg, as well as the state operas of Munich, Stuttgart, Hamburg, Dresden and Berlin.

Hasmik Papian lives in Vienna, Austria.

Repertoire

Her repertoire ranges from Mozart's *Donna Anna* (Don Giovanni), Rossini's *Mathilde* (William Tell), Halévy's *Rachel* (La Juive) and Bizet's *Micaëla* (Carmen), passing by Puccini's *Mimì* (La Bohème), *Magda* (La Rondine), Tosca, Madama Butterfly and Boito's *Margareta/ Elena* (Mefistofele) to Tchaikovsky's *Lisa* (The Queen of Spades) and Richard Wagner's *Senta* (The Flying Dutchman). It contains twelve Verdi-roles: La Traviata, *Desdemona* (Otello), Aida, *Leonora* (Il Trovatore and La forza del destino), *Elisabetta* (Don Carlo), *Elena* (I vespri siciliani), *Amelia* (Simon Boccanegra), *Elvira* (Ernani), *Lady Macbeth*, *Abigaille* (Nabucco), *Odabella* (Attila) as well as the Requiem. A central part for her is Bellini's Norma; she has appeared in this role among others at Vienna Volksoper, at the Regio of Turin, in Montreal, Baltimore, Detroit, Denver, Washington, D.C. and at the Metropolitan Opera New York, at Opéra de Marseille, Opéra de Montpellier, at the festivals Chorégies d'Orange (South of France) and Luglio Trapanese (Sicily), in Mannheim, Stuttgart, St. Gallen, Rotterdam and at De Nederlandse Opera Amsterdam. The Amsterdam production has been released on DVD in October 2006. In January 2009, she has added another bel canto role to her repertoire: Queen Elizabeth I in Donizetti's Roberto Devereux (debut at The Dallas Opera).

Artistic Appearances

Hasmik Papian has appeared in most European countries, in Israel, Lebanon (Baalbeck International Festival), Japan, Latin America (Mexico, Brazil, Chile), as well as Canada (Toronto, Montreal) and the United States where she is invited regularly (besides Washington, DC, San Francisco and the Met also Baltimore, Detroit, Cincinnati Festival and Denver, among others). She has performed with many notable conductors – such as Riccardo Muti, Valery Gergiev, Georges Prêtre, Michel Plasson, Marcello Viotti, Maurizio Arena, Myung-whun Chung, Gennady Rozhdestvensky, Plácido Domingo, Leonard Slatkin, James Morris and James Conlon. She is also very active promoting the music of fellow Armenian composers such as Komitas Vardapet, Yeranian, Kanatchian, Tchoukhadjian, Tigranian, Avet Terterian and Tigran Mansurian in her recitals. In 2006, an SACD with 36 songs of Komitas has been released, including some nine songs on German poetry recorded here for the first time ever. In 2004, she was honored with the title of the "People's Artist" of the Republic of Armenia. In 2005, she was awarded the Order of Saint Sahag-Saint Mashtots from the hands of Catholicos Garegin II of Armenia at the Holy Mother See of the Armenian Apostolic Church in Echmiadzin, for her role as a "cultural ambassador of Armenia throughout the world".

Source (edited): "http://en.wikipedia.org/wiki/Hasmik_Papian"

Komitas Vardapet

"Mokats Mirza" singing Komitas.

Soghomon Gevorki Soghomonyan - Komitas ("Սողոմոն Գևորգի Սողոմոնյան" - "Կոմիտաս" in Armenian), by Western Armenian transliteration also *Gomidas*, born on September 26 or October 8 1869 in Kütahya, Ottoman Empire, died on October 22, 1935 in Paris, France, was an Armenian priest, composer, choir leader, singer, music ethnologist, music pedagogue and musicologist. Many regard him as the founder of modern Armenian classical music.

Komitas lost his mind after witnessing the 1915 Armenian Genocide and is ranked among the Armenian martyrs of genocide.

Biography

Soghomon (Gevorki) Soghomonyan was born into a family whose members were deeply involved in music and were monolingual in Turkish. His mother died when he was one, and his father died ten years later. His grandmother looked after him until 1881 when a prelate of the local Armenian diocese went to Echmiadzin to be consecrated a bishop. The catholicos Gevork IV ordered him to bring one orphaned child to be educated at the Echmiadzin Seminary. Soghomon was chosen among 20 candidates and admitted into the seminary (where he impressed the catholicos with his singing talent) and graduated in 1893, after which he became a monk. According to church tradition, newly ordained priests are given new names, and Soghomon was renamed **Komitas** (named after the 7th century Armenian catholicos, who was also a hymn writer). Two years later he became a priest and obtained the title **Vardapet** (or **Vartabed**), meaning a *priest* or a *church scholar*.

He established and conducted the monastery choir until 1896 when he went to Berlin, enrolled the Kaiser Friedrich Wilhelm University and studied music at the private conservatory of Prof. Richard Schmidt. In 1899 he acquired the title *doctor of musicology* and returned to Echmiadzin, where he took over conducting a polyphonic male choir. He traveled extensively around the country, listening to and recording details about Armenian folk songs and dances performed in various villages. This way he collected and published some 3000 songs, many of them adapted to choir singing.

His major work is Badarak (*Divine Liturgy*), still used today as one of the two most popular musical settings of the Armenian Church liturgy or mass, which he started composing in 1892 but never completely finished due to the upcoming World War I. For the basis of the work he took chants sung by the eldest priests and upgraded it with typical ("cleaned" of foreign influences) Armenian music elements from his collected material. Today the best known version of Badarak is his favourite for a three-voiced male choir. It must be understood that the Komitas Badarak was not an original composition per se, but rather an arrangement of the pre-existing melodies in use by Armenian priests for the singing of the mass. The words certainly are not original but are the text of the Armenian mass which has been used for centuries. Armenian Church music was traditionally monophonic, but Markar Yekmalian, Komitas, and several other musician/composers in the 19th and 20th centuries arranged polyphonic versions of the pre-existing melodies. Some composers (but not Komitas or Yekmalian) created completely original musical settings of the liturgy as well.

He was the first non-European to be admitted into the International Music Society, of which he was a co-founder. He gave many lectures and performances throughout Europe, Turkey and Egypt, thus presenting till then very little known Armenian music.

From 1910 he lived and worked in Istanbul. There he established a 300-member choir *Gusan*. On April 24, 1915, the day when the Armenian Genocide officially began, he was arrested and put on a train the next day together with 180 other Armenian notables and sent to the city of Çankırı in northern Central Anatolia, at a distance of some 300 miles. His good friend, Turkish nationalist poet Mehmet Emin Yurdakul, the authoress Halide Edip, and the U.S. ambassador Henry Morgenthau intervened with the government and, by special orders from Talat Pasha, Komitas was dispatched back to the capital alongside eight other Armenians who had been deported. Armenian sources deny rumors of earlier schizophrenia or venereal disease and stress that he never fully recovered from these 15 days experience. As of autumn 1916, he was taken to a Turkish military hospital and he moved to Paris in 1919 where he died in a psychiatric clinic *Villejuif* in 1935. Next year his ashes were transferred to Yerevan and buried in the Pantheon.

Statue of Komitas in the park in front of the Yerevan State Musical Conservatory in Armenia.

Komitas on a 1969 Soviet Union postage stamp.

In 1950s his manuscripts were also transferred from Paris to Yerevan.

Badarak was first printed in 1933 in Paris and first recorded onto a digital media in 1988 in Yerevan. In collecting and publishing so many folk songs, he saved the cultural heritage of Western Armenia that otherwise would have disappeared because of the genocide. His works have been published in the Republic of Armenia in a thoroughly annotated edition by Robert Atayan. Lately, also some nine songs on German poetry, written during his stay in Berlin, have been excavated from the archives in Yerevan and interpreted by soprano Hasmik Papian.

The Yerevan State Musical Conservatory is named after Komitas. There also exists a worldwide renowned string quartet named after Komitas.

On July 6, 2008 and on the occasion of Quebec City's 400th anniversary celebration, a bronze bust of Komitas was unveiled near the Quebec National Assembly (provincial legislature, Auteuil street), in recognition of his great input to music in general and to Armenian popular and liturgical music in particular.

On September 15, 2008, the CD " Firstling Inspired by Gomidas", " Yerakhayrik", Sung by **Kevork Hadjian** was introduced and released. A 18 track compilation of Gomidas's songs including another track of non Gomidas. The cd is in stores in Armenia.

In September 2008, the CD "Gomidas Songs" sung by Isabel Bayrakdarian and accompanied by the Chamber Players of the Armenian Philharmonic and pianist Seroui Kradjian was released on the Nonesuch label. This CD is nominated for a Grammy Award in the Best Vocal Recording category. A major North American tour by Ms. Bayrakdarian in October 2008 featured the music of Komitas, with concerts in Toronto, San Francisco, Orange County, Los Angeles, Vancouver, Boston and New York's Carnegie Hall. She was accompanied by the Manitoba Chamber Orchestra conducted by Anne Manson, and pianist Seroui Kradjian. The "Remembrance Tour" was dedicated to victims of all genocides and sponsored by the International Institute for Genocide and Human Rights Studies (a division of the Zoryan Institute).

Legacy

- Central square of Ejmiatsin city is named after Komitas.
- Yerevan State Musical Conservatory

is named after Komitas Vardapet.
- Komitas Avenue, the main thoroughfare of Yerevan's Arabkir District, is named after Komitas Vardapet.
- The writers' and poets' pantheon in Yerevan is named after Komitas.

Works, editions and recordings
- *Gomidas - songs* Isabel Bayrakdarian, Serouj Kradjian (arrangements and piano), Chamber players of the Armenian Philharmonic Orchestra, conducted by Eduard Topchjan. Nonesuch, 2005

Source (edited): "http://en.wikipedia.org/wiki/Komitas_Vardapet"

Robert Kocharyan

Robert Sedraki Kocharyan (Armenian: Ռոբերտ Սեդրակի Քոչարյան, pronounced [robɛɾt' sɛdɹɑk'i kʰotʃʰɑɪjɑn]) (born August 31, 1954) was the second President of Armenia, serving from 1998 till 2008. He was previously President of Nagorno-Karabakh from 1994 to 1997 and Prime Minister of Armenia from 1997 to 1998.

Biography
Robert Kocharyan was born in Stepanakert, Nagorno-Karabakh. He received his secondary education there and from 1972 to 1974 served in the Soviet Army. He and his wife, Bella Kocharyan, have three children: Sedrak, Gayane, and Levon, all of whom were born in Stepanakert.
- 1972-1974 – served in the Soviet Army
- 1975-1976 – labor activities in different enterprises in Stepanakert and Moscow
- 1977-1982 – electrical engineering faculty of Yerevan State Polytechnic Institute. Diploma with excellence.
- 1980-1981 – worked as a mechanical engineer at the electrical engineering plant in Stepanakert
- 1981-1985 – worked at different positions at Municipal committee in Stepanakert town committee of the Komsomol Union, including the post of assistant secretary
- 1986 – instructor of town committee of Stepanakert Communist Party of the Soviet Union.
- 1987-1989 – head of Karabakh Soviet party organization of the silk factory
- 19 February 1988 – leader of the Artsakh movement, which fought for secession from the Azerbaijan Soviet Socialist Republic and for later union with Armenia; member of group *Krunk*; led the *Miatsum* organization
- 1989-1995 – twice elected as a deputy of Supreme Council of Republic of Armenia, and member of the Presidium of the Supreme Soviet
- 1991-1992 deputy of the Supreme Union of the Nagorno-Karabakh Republic in its first convocation

Presidency
After the resignation of his predecessor Levon Ter-Petrossian, Kocharyan was elected Armenia's second President on March 30, 1998, defeating his main rival, Karen Demirchyan, in an early presidential election marred by irregularities and violations by both sides as reported by international electoral observers. Complaints included that Kocharyan had not been an Armenian citizen for ten years as required by the constitution., even though it would have been impossible for him to be a 10 year citizen of a republic that was less than 7 years old; however, the Armenian constitution recognized the Armenian SSR as it predecessor state.

During his presidency, several opposition leaders in the Armenian Parliament and the Prime Minister of Armenia were killed by gunmen in an episode known as the 1999 Armenian parliament shooting. And Kocharyan himself negotiated with terrorists to lease the MP hostages. It is widely believed by Armenians at large that Kocharyan is responsible for the parliament shooting.

2003 election
The 2003 Armenian Presidential election on 19 February and 5 March 2003. No candidate received a majority in the first round of the election with the incumbent President Kocharyan winning slightly under 50% of the vote. Therefore a second round was held and Kocharyan defeated Stepan Demirchyan with official results showed him winning just over 67% of the vote.

In both rounds, electoral observers from the Organization for Security and Co-operation in Europe reported significant amounts of electoral fraud by Demirchyan's supporters and numerous supporters of Demirchyan were arrested before the second round took place. Demirchyan described the election as having being rigged and called on his supporters to rally against the results. Tens of thousands of Armenians protested in the days after the election against the results and called on President Kocharyan to step down. However Kocharyn was sworn in for a second term in early April and the constitutional court upheld the election, while recommending that a referendum be held within a year to confirm the election result.

2008 election
A presidential election was held in Armenia on 19 February 2008. The incumbent President Kocharyan, who was ineligible for a third consecutive term, backed the candidacy of Prime Minister of Armenia Serzh Sargsyan.

Following the election result, protests organized by supporters of unsuccessful candidate Levon Ter-Petrossian began in Yerevan's Freedom Square and accompanied by mass disorders. On March 1, the demonstrators were lawfully dispersed by police and military forces. 10 people was killed during skirmishes between police and aggressive crowd, and President Kocharyan declared a 20-day state of emergency. This was followed by mass arrests and purges of prominent members of the opposition who made disorders and damaged life and property of citizens, as well as a de facto ban on any further anti-government protests. Kocharyan was recognized as successful president

Foreign policy

President Vladimir Putin with Armenian President Robert Kocharyan

President George W. Bush with Armenian President Robert Kocharyan

As President, Kocharyan continued to negotiate a peaceful resolution with Azerbaijani President Ilham Aliyev on the status of Nagorno-Karabakh. Talks between Aliyev and Kocharyan were held in September 2004 in Astana, Kazakhstan, on the sidelines of the Commonwealth of Independent States (CIS) summit. Reportedly, one of the suggestions put forward was the withdrawal of Armenian forces from the Azeri territories adjacent to Nagorno-Karabakh, and holding referendums (plebiscites) in Nagorno-Karabakh and Azerbaijan proper regarding the future status of the region. On February 10–11, 2006, Kocharyan and Aliyev met in Rambouillet, France to discuss the fundamental principles of a settlement to the conflict, including the withdrawal of troops, formation of international peace keeping troops, and the status of Nagorno-Karabakh.

During the weeks and days before the talks in France, OSCE Minsk Group co-chairmen expressed cautious optimism that some form of an agreement was possible. French President Jacques Chirac met with both leaders separately and expressed hope that the talks would be fruitful. Contrary to the initial optimism, the Rambouillet talks did not produce any agreement, with key issues such as the status of Nagorno-Karabakh and whether Armenian troops would withdraw from Kalbajar still being contentious. The next session of the talks was held in March 2006 in Washington, D.C. Russian President, Vladimir Putin applied pressure to both parties to settle the disputes. Later in 2006 there was a meeting of the Armenian and Azerbaijani Presidents in Minsk on 28 November and ministerial meetings were held in Moscow. "These talks did not initiate any progress, but I hope that the time for a solution will come" said Peter Semneby, EU envoy for the South Caucasus.

In September 2006, in his congratulatory message on the occasion of 15th anniversary of Nagorno-Karabakh Republic, Kocharyan said "The Karabakhi people made their historic choice, defended their national interests in the war that was forced upon them. Today, they are building a free and independent state." The accompanying message said that the duty of the Republic of Armenia and all Armenians is to contribute to the strengthening and development of Nagorno-Karabakh, as well as to the international recognition of the republic's independence.

Source (edited): "http://en.wikipedia.org/wiki/Robert_Kocharyan"

Serzh Sargsyan

Serzh Azati Sargsyan (Armenian: Սերժ Ազատի Սարգսյան, born June 30, 1954) is the third President of Armenia. He won the February 2008 presidential election with the backing of the conservative Republican Party of Armenia, a party in which he serves as chairman, and took office in April 2008. He is of no relation to the current Prime Minister of Armenia Tigran Sargsyan.

Personal life

Serzh Sargsyan was born on June 30, 1954 in Stepanakert, Azerbaijan SSR, USSR. He was admitted to Yerevan State University in 1971, served in the Soviet Armed Forces during 1971-72, and graduated from the Philological Department of Yerevan State University in 1979. In 1983, he married his wife, Rita. They have two daughters, Anush and Satenik, and one granddaughter, Mariam. He is the chairman of the Chess Federation of Armenia. In addition to his native Armenian, he is fluent in Russian, English and Azeri, but he has not spoken Azeri for 20 years.

Early career

Sargsyan's career began in 1975 at the Electrical Devices Factory in Yerevan, where he worked as a metal turner until 1979 when he became head of the Stepanakert City Communist Party Youth Association Committee. Then served as second secretary, first secretary, the Stepanakert City Committee Propaganda Division Head, the Nagorno-Karabakh Regional Committee Communist Organizations' Unit Instructor, and finally as the assistant to Genrikh Poghosyan, the First Secretary of the Nagorno-Karabakh Regional Committee.

As tensions rose over Nagorno-Karabakh between Armenians and Azerbaijanis, Sargsyan became chairman of the Nagorno-Karabakh Republic Self-Defense Forces Committee and was subsequently elected to the Supreme Council of Armenia in 1990. He organized several battles in the Nagorno-Karabakh War and is considered to be one of the founders of

Nagorno-Karabakh's and Armenia's armed forces. He became the Armenian defense minister in 1993, head of Armenian state security department in 1995 and minister of national security in 1996. In 1999, he became Robert Kocharyan's chief of staff, then secretary of the national security council, defense minister, and prime minister in 2007.

2008 presidential election

Sargsyan, with President Kocharyan's backing, was viewed as the strongest contender for the post of the President of Armenia in the February 2008 presidential election. Full provisional results showed him winning about 53% of the vote, a first round majority, well ahead of second place candidate Levon Ter-Petrossian. Ter-Petrossian's supporters, disputing the official results, held large protests in Yerevan for over a week following the election, until they were violently broken up by police on March 1; ten people were killed, and a state of emergency was imposed for 20 days, ending on March 20, 2008.

Presidency

Serzh Sargsyan was sworn in as President inside the Yerevan Opera House on April 9. Referring to the "painful events" that followed the election, he "urge[d] everybody to look forward, together, to seek and find the way for reconciliation, development, and future of Armenia." He appointed Tigran Sargsyan, who had been the Chairman of the Central Bank and is not a member of a political party, as Prime Minister. Vazgen Manukyan, a former member of the Karabakh Committee and a prominent oppositionist, stated that he is optimistic and "will do everything to help this government become successful". On April 18, Sargsyan launched an unusually blistering attack on the Armenian customs, saying that "corruption within its ranks is 'thriving' and hampering the countrys economic development." He later authorized an opposition to take place in Yerevan and pledged to comply with the Council of Europe's demands for an end to the government's crackdown on the opposition.

Foreign policy

Sargsyan initially stated that he will continue Armenia's policy towards Turkey, to normalize relations without any preconditions while continuing to strive for international recognition of the 1915 Armenian Genocide. On October 10, 2009, however, by signing the Turkish-Armenian protocols on the establishment of diplomatic relations, he most notably accepted a precondition in regards to the veracity of the Armenian genocide, in that he accepted the proposal of studying the issue through a commission. Moreover, with his acceptance of the current Turkish-Armenian border, he neglected Armenian demands for Western Armenia, which are supported by the Treaty of Sevres. He also stated that "Armenia's possible recognition of Kosovo's independence will not strain the Armenian-Russian relations" but also noted that the "Kosovo recognition issue needs serious discussion ... Armenia has always been an adherent to the right of nations to self-determination and in this aspect we welcome Kosovo's independence."

Sargsyan made his first address in front of the 63rd session of the United Nations General Assembly in New York on September 25, 2008. In his address he referenced the 2008 South Ossetia conflict and emphasized the need for the United Nations to help bring peaceful resolution to armed conflicts around the world, including the one in Nagorno-Karabakh. He also mentioned how Azerbaijan's military buildup along with increasing war rhetoric and threats risked causing renewed problems in the South Caucasus.

Protests

Major protests against Sargsyan's regime erupted in 2011, with the president's 2008 rival Levon Ter-Petrossian at their helm. In a concession to protesters, Sargsyan said on 20 April 2011 that the government would recommit to a thorough investigation of the post-election violence of three years prior.

Honors

Serzh Sargsyan has thus far been conferred the following honors:
- Order of first Degree "Martakan Khach" ("Combat Cross")
- Hero of Artsakh
- Knight of "Voske Artsiv" (Golden Eagle) order
- Order of "Tigran Mets"

Other details

Other transcriptions of his given name are *Serge* and *Serj,* of the surname *Sarkissian, Sarkisyan, Sargsyan, Sarkissyan,* the transliteration is *Serž Azati Sargsyan* (see Romanization of Armenian).

Source (edited): "http://en.wikipedia.org/wiki/Serzh_Sargsyan"

Tiridates III of Armenia

Tiridates III (or **Trdat III**; Armenian: Տրդատ Գ; 250 – c. 330) was the king of Arsacid Armenia (285-339), and is also known as **Tiridates the Great** Տրդատ Մեծ; some scholars incorrectly refer to him as Tiridates IV as a result of the fact that Tiridates I of Armenia reigned twice). In 301, Tiridates proclaimed Christianity as the state religion of Armenia, making the Armenian kingdom the first state to officially embrace Christianity. He is recognized as a saint by the Armenian Apostolic Church.

Early Childhood

Tiridates III was the son of Khosrov II of Armenia, the latter being assassinated in 252 by a Parthian agent named Anak under orders from Ardashir I. Anak was captured and executed along with most of his family, while two of his sons one of whom was Saint Gregory the Illuminator were sheltered in Caesaria. Being the only surviving heir to the throne, Tiridates was quickly taken away to Rome soon after his father's assassination, while still an infant. He was educated in Rome and was well skilled in languages and military tactics; in addition, he firmly understood and appreciated Roman law.

Kingship

Grigor Illuminator baptizes Tiridates III of Armenia

In 270 AD the Roman emperor Aurelian engaged the Sassanids, who had now replaced the Parthians, on the eastern front and he was able to drive them back. Tiridates, as the true heir to the now Persian-occupied Armenian throne, came to Armenia and quickly raised an army and drove the enemy out in 287 AD. The Roman-Armenian alliance grew stronger, especially while Diocletian ruled the empire. This can be attributed to the upbringing of Tiridates, the consistent Persian aggressions, and the murder of his father by Anak. With Diocletian's help, Tiridates pushed the Persians out of Armenia. In 299, Diocletian left the Armenian state in a quasi-independent and protectorate status possibly to use it as a buffer in case of a Persian attack.

Conversion

The baptism of Tiridates III.

The traditional story of the conversion of the king and the nation tells of how Gregory the Illuminator, the son of Anak, was a Christian convert who, feeling guilt for his own father's sin, joined the Armenian army and worked as a secretary to the king. Christianity in Armenia had a strong footing by the end of the 3rd century AD but the nation by and large still followed Zoroastrianism. Tiridates III was no exception as he too worshiped various ancient gods. During a pagan religious ceremony Tiridates III ordered Gregory to place a flower wreath at the foot of the statue of the goddess Anahit in Eriza. Gregory refused, proclaiming his Christian faith. This act infuriated the king. His fury was only exacerbated when several individuals declared that Gregory was, in fact, the son of Anak, the traitor who had killed Tiridates's father. Gregory was tortured and finally thrown in Khor Virap, a deep underground dungeon.

During the years of Gregory's imprisonment, a group of virgin nuns, led by Gayane, came to Armenia as they fled the Roman persecution of their Christian faith. Tiridates III heard about the group and the legendary beauty of one of its members, Rhipsime (also Hripsime or Ripsime). He brought them to the palace and demanded to marry the beautiful virgin; she refused. The king had the whole group tortured and killed. After this event, he fell ill and according to legend, adopted the behavior of a wild boar, aimlessly wandering around in the forest. The king's sister, Xosroviduxt, had a dream wherein Gregory was still alive in the dungeon and he was the only one able to cure the king. At this point it had been 13 years since his imprisonment, and the odds of him being alive were slim. But they retrieved him and despite being incredibly malnourished he was still alive. He was reportedly kept alive by a kindhearted woman that threw a loaf of bread down in Khor Virap everyday for him.

Tiridates was brought to Gregory, and was miraculously cured of his illness in 301 AD. Persuaded by the power of the cure, the king immediately proclaimed Christianity the official state religion. And so, Armenia became the first nation to officially adopt Christianity. Tiridates III appointed Gregory as Catholicos of the Armenian Apostolic Church.

Rest of reign

The switch from the traditional pagan Armenian religion to Christianity was not an easy one. Tiridates often used force to impose this new faith upon the people and many armed conflicts ensued, because polytheism was deeply rooted in the Armenian people. An actual battle took place between the king's forces and the pagan camp, resulting in the weakening of polytheistic military strength. Tiridates thus spent the rest of his life trying to eliminate all ancient beliefs and in doing so destroyed countless statues, temples and written documents. As a result, little is known from local sources about ancient Armenian history and culture. The king worked feverishly to spread the faith and died in 330 AD.

According to the Armenian historian Movses Khorenatsi, several members of the nakharar families conspired against

Husik Santurjan

Husik Santurjan (1920 – February 1, 2011) was an archbishop of the Armenian Apostolic Church.

Born in Turkey, Santurjan was ordained a priest in 1956 and a bishop in 1962 for the Armenian Apostolic Church.

Source (edited): "http://en.wikipedia.org/wiki/Husik_Santurjan"

Sebouh Chouldjian

Bishop Sebouh Chouldjian (born **Haik Sarkis Chouldjian**, Armenian: Սեպուհ եպիսկոպոս Չուլջյան, Turkish: *Episkopos Sebuh Çulcuyan*, Russian: Епископ Сепух Чулджян, also **Sebuh, Sepouh, Sepuh, Chuljian, Tchuljian, Chuljyan, Çulciyan**) is the Primate of the Diocese of Gougark of the Holy Armenian Apostolic Church.

Biography

Bishop Sebouh was born on March 24, 1959 in Malatya, Turkey. He received his primary education at the Nersisian College of Istanbul. In 1969, his family repatriated to Armenia and settled in the city of Gyumri, where he continued and finished his primary education.

In 1978 he entered the Gevorkian Theological Seminary at the Mother See of Holy Etchmiadzin. He was ordained to the diaconate in 1985, by the Grand Sacristan of the Mother See of Holy Etchmiadzin, Archbishop Hoosik Santourian. He successfully defended his final thesis entitled "*The Translation Works of Lukas of Kharpert*" in March, 1986. Upon his graduation from the seminary he was appointed to serve in the Secretariat of the Pontifical Administration.

He was ordained as a celibate priest by Archbishop Nerses Pozapalian on June 7, 1987, the Feast of Pentecost, and given the priestly name Sebouh. Following his ordination, he continued his service in the Pontifical Administration.

By the appointment of Vazgen I, Catholicos of All Armenians, he served as the Vice Dean of the Gevorkian Theological Seminary at the Mother See of Holy Etchmiadzin in September, 1987. In November, 1989, he successfully defended his doctoral thesis entitled "*The Fast in the Armenian Apostolic Church*," and received the rank of Archimandrite (Vardapet).

In 1990, Vazgen I appointed Father Sebouh to serve as the spiritual pastor of the Armenians of Geneva, Switzerland. He returned to Armenia in 1991 to serve as the Vicar of the Diocese of Shirak.

After the Republic of Armenia gained independence, vast administrative tasks were placed on the Armenian Church. In the summer of 1993, Father Sebouh worked closely with Archbishop Hovnan Derderian (the then primate of the Diocese of Canada) and Ronald Alepian to organize the first mission of Canadian Youth Mission to Armenia (CYMA). In June 1995, Father Sebouh was appointed to serve as the Director of the Reserve Stewardship Inventory Committee of the Armenian Church. Also in that same year, he was appointed to serve as the Director of the committee responsible for tracking the return and receipt of all previously confiscated church buildings, land and construction projects (most of the churches, buildings, structures and properties belonging to the Church had been seized by the State during the time of the Soviet Regime).

In 1996, he served as the representative of the Armenian Church on the Humanitarian Aid Central Committee of the Republic of Armenia. On June 3, 1996, by the Pontifical Encyclical of the Karekin I, Catholicos of All Armenians, Father Sebouh he was appointed to serve as the Primate of the Diocese of Gougark.

Father Sebouh was consecrated as bishop by Catholicos Karekin I on June 15, 1997. He was a member of the Supreme Spiritual Council of the Armenian Church during 2000-2007.

Bishop Sebouh presently serves as the Primate of the Diocese of Gougark in Armenia.

Co-Patriarch Candidacy (2010)

Bishop Sebouh Chouldjian was one of the three candidates for the Co-Patriarch at the Armenian Patriarchate of Constantinople in 2010.

Mesrop II Mutafyan, the Armenian Patriarch of Constantinople was diagnosed with Alzheimer's disease in July, 2008, and was incapable of running the Patriarchate since then. This led the Armenian community to a painful condition of uncertainty. In late 2009, the Patriarchate's Religious Council wrote to the Turkish government seeking permission to elect a coadjutor (co-Patriarch).

Among the main ideas proposed by Bishop Sebouh as a candidate was that the Armenian Patriarchate of Constantinople should become a spiritual and cultural bridge among Yerevan, Ankara and the Armenian Diaspora. He paid particular attention to the importance of dialogue among Armenians and between Turkish and Armenian people.

On February 10–17, 2010 Bishop Sebouh visited Istanbul, Turkey to have meetings with the Armenian community of Istanbul. During his meetings and interviews he urged to continue Hrant Dink's way (i.e. dialogue between Armenian and Turkish people) and keep Armenian Patriarchate free from politics.

On June 29, 2010 the government of Turkey made a decision to reject the request of the Armenian community of Turkey to allow co-patriarch elections.

The Turkish Government said that they did not find the elections of either patriarch or co-patriarch reasonable and allowed carrying out only the elections of Patriarchal Locum Tenens. Hours later Archbishop Shahan Svajian - the that time Locum Tenens, resigned and the Spiritual council of the Patriarchate elected Archbishop Aram Ateshian a new Patriarchal Locum Tenens. However, according to some experts, the Armenian Community of Turkey was inclined to elect Bishop Sebouh Chouldjian (citizen of Armenia) as their spiritual leader which was disallowed by the Turkish government after unsuccessful negotiations of Armenia-Turkey reconciliation. Despite the protests of the Armenian community representatives, it will hardly be possible to hold new patriarch elections as long as the current patriarch Mesrop II is alive.

Later, in his letter to the Armenian Community of Turkey from July 15, 2010 Bishop Sebouh mentioned that interference of Turkey's Government was in contradiction with the adopted new policy on dealing with ethnic minorities. "We continue to hope that this is not the manner of actions of Erdoğan's government, but that of the stationary state sub-agencies, which hamper the democratic development of Turkey with their old mentality". Bishop Sebouh said it was the moral obligation of Archbishop Aram Ateshian to send a new letter to the Turkey's Government with request to hold the elections of Co-Patriarch.

Honors and awards

Bishop Sebouh is member of the Armenian branch of the International Academy of Natural and Social Sciences (since 2000).

He holds Fridtjof Nansen Golden Medal (2005), Republic of Armenia Prime Minister's Medal for vast contribution in development of state-church relations (2006), Hayrenik Gold Medal (2010).

On March 24, 2009, Prime Minister of the Republic of Armenia Tigran Sargsyan warmly congratulated Bishop Sebouh on the occasion of the 50 anniversary of birthday. In his message he emphasized Bishop Sebouh's input in organizing Christian education, revivification of church life and restoration of ethnic and spiritual identity of the Armenian nation.

Bishop Sebouh Chouldjian

Bishop Sebouh during Liturgy

Bishop Sebouh with representatives of Istanbul Armenian Community

Bishop Sebouh at the grave of Hrant Dink in Istanbul, Turkey

Bishop Sebouh blessing the faithful

Bishop Sebouh washing the feet of children during the Washing of Feet ceremony

See also

- Photo gallery of the meeting of the members of the Organization of Istanbul Armenians with Bishop Sebouh at oia.net.

Source (edited): "http://en.wikipedia.org/wiki/Sebouh_Chouldjian"

Abraham III of Armenia

Catholicos Abraham III (also **Abraham of Crete** or **Abraham Kretatsi**) was the Catholicos of the Armenian Apostolic Church between 1734 and 1737. Born in Heraklion, Crete, to a Greek mother, he was bishop of Rodosto, Thrace and then Armenian prelate of Thrace from 1708-1734. At this time he went on a pilgrimage to eastern Armenia, at that time under Persian rule, which now make up the area of modern day Armenia and Nakhichevan. Abraham is said to have become Catholicos by chance, because while he was on his pilgrimage to Etchmiadzin Catholicos Abraham II died. Abraham of Crete had impressed many with his religious devotion during his stay there, and so they decided unanimously to elect him the new Catholicos. Abraham III was old at this point and unfamiliar in the workings of Etchmiadzin, so he protested, but despite that in November 1734 he was named the 110th Catholicos of the Armenian Church.

Abraham III came to the throne at a volatile time in the region. Nader Shah of Persia was reconquesting areas which had been lost by his predecessors to the Ottomans including Armenia. Abraham wrote a chronicle of Nader's campaign against the Turks and of his coronation as Shah when in the area. It is a helpful history because it is one of the few non-Persian sources about these years in the Transcaucasus. Abraham wrote that many villages had been left destitute by the Ottoman invasion and that the area was suffering greatly. Abraham was invited as a guest of honor at Nader's coronation and Armenian princes were granted autonomy. Abraham recorded detailed conversations he had with the Shah, most likely partly to serve as a record of the many privileges granted to Armenians by the shah and to serve as an example to the Ottomans who also ruled over a large Armenian population. Nader Shah visited the Armenian mother church of Etchmiadzin and reconfirmed its tax-exempt status.

Abraham III died in April 1737 at Etchmiadzin and was buried there after his short but successful reign.

Source (edited): "http://en.wikipedia.org/wiki/Abraham_III_of_Armenia"

Ananias I of Armenia

Catholicos Ananias I was the Catholicos of the Armenian Apostolic Church between 949 and 968.

His predecessor Yeghishe had been deposed as Catholicos and by church regulations no one could be elected during his lifetime. The office was held by a deputy until Yeghishe died two years later and Ananias of Varagavank became pontiff. Catholicos Ananias moved the seat of the Catholicosate from Vaspurakan at Akhtamar to the town of Arghina. He coronated Ashot III in 961 at his new capital nearby of Ani. In 958 the Catholicos ended the schism of the bishop of Syunik, who was supported by the Catholicos of Albania, at the Council of Kapan by consecrating its new metropolitan. This period showed a great deal of involvement of the king in church activities. A relative of Ananias later became Catholicos Khachig I of Armenia.

Source (edited): "http://en.wikipedia.org/wiki/Ananias_I_of_Armenia"

Asdvadzadur of Armenia

Catholicos Asdvadzadur was the Catholicos of the Armenian Apostolic Church between 1715 and 1725.

As Catholicos, he secured an alliance with Christian Peter the Great of Russia for aid against the expansionist Muslim powers of the Ottoman Empire and Persia prior to the Russo-Persian War.

Tombstone of Astvadzadur I, Catholicos of All Armenians, at St. Hripsime church.

He is buried at St. Hripsime Church, Echmiadzin.

Source (edited): "http://en.wikipedia.org/wiki/Asdvadzadur_of_Armenia"

Aspuraces I

Aspuraces I (Armenian: Ասպուրակէս Ա. Մանազկերտցի) was a catholicos of the Armenian Apostolic Church. He reigned from 381 to 386 AD and third of three catholicoi from the Albaniosid Dynasty.

Source (edited): "http://en.wikipedia. org/wiki/Aspuraces_I"

Bartholomew the Apostle

Bartholomew was one of the Twelve Apostles of Jesus, and is usually identified as Nathaniel (alternate spelling: Nathanael) (mentioned in the first chapter of John's Gospel). He was introduced to Christ through St. Philip, another of the twelve apostles as per (John 1:43-51), where the name Nathaniel first appears. He is also mentioned as "Nathaniel of Cana in Galilee" in (John 21:1). The name Nathaniel is the one used for him in St. John's Gospel. The relationship between St. Philip and Nathaniel is noted as per John 1:43-51.

Bartholomew (Greek: Βαρθολομαίος, transliterated "Bartholomaios") comes from the Aramaic *bar-Tôlmay* (בר-תולמי), meaning *son of Tolmay* (Ptolemy) or *son of the furrows* (perhaps a ploughman).

According to the Synaxarium of the Coptic Orthodox Church [The Church of Alexandria, the ancient Church of Egypt, one of the Oldest in Christianity], his martyrdom is commemorated on the 1st day of the Coptic Calendar (1st day of the month of "Thout"), which currently falls on September 11 [this corresponds to August 29 in the Gregorian Calendar, due to the current 13 day offset between the Julian and Gregorian Calendars]. The festival in August has been a traditional occasion for markets and fairs, such as the Bartholomew Fair held in Smithfield, London since the Middle Ages that served as the scene for Ben Jonson's homonymous comedy.

Source (edited): "http://en.wikipedia. org/wiki/Bartholomew_the_Apostle"

Basil of Ani

Basil of Ani or **Basil Pahlavuni** (Armenian: Բարսեղ Փահլավունի; Barsegh Pahlavuni; died 13 November 1113 AD) was Armenian Catholicoi of Cilicia from 1105 to 1113.

Basil was the nephew of Catholicos Gregory II the Martyrophile. He was the bishop of Seljuk-occupied Ani from 1081 to 1105. In 1090 he was appointed the bishop of Marash which enjoyed the support of Philaretos Brachamios. In 1103 he visited Edessa where he was received by Baldwin II magnificently. When Vahram (birthname of Catholicos Gregory II) died on the 5th December, 1105 in Karmir Vank (Red Monastery), in the principality of Kesun, he was in charge of the burial and was elected as the new Catholikos.

He moved his residence several times from Zamintia (Tzamandos) to the confines of Cilicia, then being filled with Armenian refugees, fleeing from Seljuk invasions. The monastery of Shugur on the Orontes River, in Sev Ler (Amanus, Black Mountains), became a favorite home for Basil. He died on 13 November 1113 when a balcony accidentally collapsed. His 18-year-old nephew Gregory III Pahlavuni (1113–1166) became his successor.

Source (edited): "http://en.wikipedia. org/wiki/Basil_of_Ani"

Catholicos of All Armenians

The **Catholicos of All Armenians** (plural *Catholicoi*, due to its Greek origin) is the chief bishop of Armenia's national church, the Armenian Apostolic Church. It is one of the Oriental Orthodox churches that do not accept the decisions of the Council of Chalcedon. The first Catholicos of All Armenians was Saint Gregory the Illuminator. According to tradition, it was the apostles Saint Thaddeus and Saint Bartholomew, who brought Christianity to Armenia in the 1st century.

The Supreme Spiritual and Administrative leader of the Armenian Church is the Supreme Patriarch and Catholicos of All Armenians, who is the worldwide spiritual leader of the Nation, for Armenians both in Armenia and dispersed throughout the world. He is Chief Shepherd and Pontiff to the Armenian faithful. The spiritual and administrative headquarters of the Armenian Church, the Mother See of Holy Etchmiadzin, located in the city of Vagharshapat, Republic of Armenia, was established in 301 AD

Source (edited): "http://en.wikipedia. org/wiki/Catholicos_of_All_Armenians"

Christopher II of Armenia

Christopher II, was the Catholicos of Armenia from 628 through 630. According to the historian Sebeos 'he proved to be an arrogant and impious man whose tongue was as sharp as a sword'. Due to this accusations were brought against him and the bishops and princes of the land were assembled to undertake an investigation. Two men from Christopher's family came to the trial and testified against him, as he had caused strife amongst his brothers as well. He was found guilty and he was defrocked from the priesthood and removed from the patriarchal throne. Ezr from the district of Nig was quickly enthroned to replace him who was said to have been a humble man, much the opposite of Christopher.

Source (edited): "http://en.wikipedia.org/wiki/Christopher_II_of_Armenia"

Daniel I of Armenia

Daniel I of Armenia (Armenian: Դանիէլ Ա.) was a Syrian who became Catholicos in Armenia's Holy Apostolic Church after the reign of four hereditary Parthian catholicoi (St. Gregory I the Enlightener, his son St. Aristaces I, St. Vrtanes I and St. Husik I. He ruled symbolically less than one year in 347 AD and was succeedd by Pharen I of Armenia of the Ashishatts Dynasty.

Source (edited): "http://en.wikipedia.org/wiki/Daniel_I_of_Armenia"

David I of Armenia

Catholicos David I was the Catholicos of the Armenian Apostolic Church between 728 and 741. He was from Aramus (then called Aramonk) in the district of Kotayk. He moved the Holy See from Dvin to Aramonk due to Dvin's having fallen into Arab hands and problems which resulted from that. Catholicos David built a church and patriarchal residence there, near which he was buried upon his death.

Source (edited): "http://en.wikipedia.org/wiki/David_I_of_Armenia"

Dertad I

Catholicos Dertad I was the Catholicos of the Armenian Apostolic Church between 741 and 764. According to the historian Kirakos Ganjaketsi, Dertad was from Otmus village and was a 'modest, blessed man, radiant in all virtue'. He reigned in a time of relative peace with a break in the Arab invasions.

Source (edited): "http://en.wikipedia.org/wiki/Dertad_I"

Garabed II of Armenia

Catholicos Garabed II Oolnetzi was the Catholicos of the Armenian Apostolic Church between 1725 and 1729.

He was elected Catholicos in Constantinople by the community and Patriarch there. He was seen by the Ottoman leaders as a trusted bridge to establish favorable relations with the new Ottoman administration of Eastern Armenia. He wrote a letter to the Pope signifying his obedience to the Roman Catholic church.

Tombstone of Garabed II, Catholicos of All Armenians, at St. Hripsime church

He is buried at St. Hripsime Church, Echmiadzin.

Source (edited): "http://en.wikipedia.org/wiki/Garabed_II_of_Armenia"

George II of Armenia

Catholicos George II of Garni, **Kevork II** in Armenian, was the Catholicos of the Armenian Apostolic Church between 877 and 897. Hovhannes Draskhanakerttsi calls him an honorable man who was selected from the Catholicos's household by Prince Ashot I of Armenia to succeed Patriarch Zacharias. George anointed and crowned Ashot I when he was declared King of Armenia in 884. Upon King Ashot's death, George went to Bagaran to preside over his funeral. Ashot's heir Smbat I, who had been away at war, missed his father's funeral and was very grieved. Catholicos George went to comfort King Smbat at Yerazgavors, where he would later also preside at his coronation. This enraged the sparapet Abas who is said to have spread false rumors about the Catholicos in an attempt to bring him down. Abas tried to convince a holy man named Mashdotz from Sevanavank to join his conspiracy against the Catholicos and said he would name him Catholicos if it was successful. Mashdotz wrote a long letter in response, rejecting the offer to rebel against the Catholicos and chided Abas for his attempt. Hovhannes Draskhanakerttsi reports at this point Abas was struck by an illness and died, as if by divine wrath, and the other conspirators repented to the Catholicos out of fear. Around this time Dvin was hit by an earthquake, as it had been during Patriarch Zacharias's time, but this time it destroyed the church of the Catholicosate, as well as many other buildings and people. Afshin, the Caliph's representative in Atropatene, who had made an agreement of friendship with Smbat, was worried at various victories Smbat was having and that he might not remain faithful to their agreement if he became too strong. Afshin invaded Armenia and reached Dvin. War broke out and Catholicos George went to meet Afshin in an attempt to get him to reconsider. Afshin attempted to get George to bring King Smbat to him for a discussion, but the nakharars advised him not to go for fear of a trap. They also begged the Catholicos not to return to Afshin but George insisted. Afshin saw that the Catholicos could not bring the King to him so he had George bound with iron fetters and handcuffs. Afshin marched against King Smbat and they met in battle, after which they agreed that Smbat would pay royal taxes to Afshin and reconfirm his oath. Afshin did not return the Catholicos however, who remained bound and suffered greatly. After two months of torture and prayers a ransom was demanded for the Catholicos's release. His bishops, including Hovhannes Draskhanakerttsi, appraoched the nakhararas and the ransom was gathered. George had been brought to Paytakaran where the ransom was paid and he was returned to Armenia. Catholicos George died in Vaspurakan in 897 and his body was taken to the cemetery of Joroy Vank in Tosp. The king of his associates then elected Mashdotz to succeed him, the same Mashdotz who had previously rejected the chance to overthrow his predecessor.

Source (edited): "http://en.wikipedia.org/wiki/George_II_of_Armenia"

George VI of Armenia

George VI of Armenia (December 2, 1868 - May 9, 1954) was the Catholicos of the Armenian Apostolic Church from 1945 to 1954.

Tombstone of George VI, Catholicos of All Armenians, at Mother Cathedral of Holy Etchmiadzin

George VI is buried near Mother Cathedral of Holy Etchmiadzin.

Source (edited): "http://en.wikipedia.org/wiki/George_VI_of_Armenia"

Gomidas

Gomidas, also known as Komitas, bishop of Taron, was the Catholicos of Armenia from 615 through 628. He is also known to have been a hymn writer. He pulled down the original chapel and rebuilt the St. Hripsime Church at Etchmiadzin as it is seen today.

Komitas was also the editor of the collection of Armenian translations of patristic texts (including extracts from lost texts, e.g. Timothy Aelurus) known as the Seal of Faith.

Source (edited): "http://en.wikipedia.org/wiki/Gomidas"

Gregory II the Martyrophile

Gregory II the Martyrophile was the Catholicos of the Armenian Apostolic Church between 1066 and 1105.

On the death of Khachig II the Byzantines had hoped to leave Armenia without a pontiff for good, part of an effort to subdue them as a people and assimilate them into the Greek rite. However, Mary the daughter of King Gagik-Abas of Kars was a favorite of Byzantine Empress Eudokia Makrembolitissa and obtained through her influence the permission to fill the empty seat. A meeting of the clergy elected Gregory the Martyrophile, son of Gregorius Magistratus, as pontiff. Gregory had been engaged in literary pursuits from a young age, had been honored by the emperor as a Duke, and had succeeded his father on his death as governor of Mesopotamia. He had grown tired of the world and embraced a monastic life. On his election he changed his original name of Vahram to Gregory in honor of Gregory the Illuminator. His name the Martyrophile came from his having compiled the memoirs of Christian martyrs.

The Byzantine army invaded again and Gregory abdicated in 1071 since he was unable to stave off these problems. He appointed a monk George Lorensis as his successor and retired to a mountain around Tarsus. He was still regarded by the Armenian people as pontiff however and they referred to him for advice. Lorensis was offended by this and took imprudent measures as a response, at which point the clergy met at Gregory's retreat and deposed Lorensis. He had reigned for two years and Gregory resumed the office officially. At this same time a monk named Sarkis exercised control in his local region as pontiff and was succeeded by Theodorus, but none of them nor Lorensis are considered canon pontiffs. Shortly after regaining his position as pontiff around 1074, Gregory made a visit to Ani which at that point was in the hands of the Persians and resided there a few months. He then returned home and wrote a letter to Pope Gregory VII, who responded in a friendly manner. Gregory II traveled to Rome to visit the Pope who was very curious to learn about the Armenian church. After a few months, Gregory II then made pilgrimage to Jerusalem and then went to Memphis, Egypt where he lived for a year. He appointed a nephew of his, Gregorius, as prelate at Memphis and then finally returned home.

With Gregory II living in Tarsus, the eastern Armenians considered themselves without a pontiff and obtained his sanction to elect his nephew, Parsegh bishop of Ani, as their pontiff. Two years later, a prince who settled in Marash elected Paul, abbot of Varagavank, to be considered pontiff of the church in that region. This means there were now four pontiffs of the Armenian church: Gregory II in the region of Mount Tarsus, Parsegh his nephew in Ani for the eastern Armenians, the previously-mentioned Theodorus, and Paul in Marash. There was much enmity between them and the cause of much confusion. Paul saw this and decided to relinquish his seat and retire to his convent, at which time the nation at large recognized Gregory II alone as pontiff, with Parsegh as his deputy. In 1087 Parsegh deposed Theodorus and settled at Edessa.

In 1103, after many requests, Gregory II finally accepted the invitation of Basil the Sly to move his residence to Rapan, in the vicinity of the city of Cheson, to spend his last years. As he left his Tarsus monastery, he took with him wards Gregory III of Cilicia and Nerses IV the Graceful, in whom he recognized future greatness. He entrusted the two preteens to the care of his nephew and deputy Parsegh as well as to his host Basil, and stated that on his death Parsegh should be made Catholicos and after him should follow young Gregory. He died shortly after and was buried there at the red convent at Rapan near Cheson.

Source (edited): "http://en.wikipedia.org/wiki/Gregory_II_the_Martyrophile"

Gregory the Illuminator

Saint Gregory the Illuminator or **Saint Gregory the Enlightener** (Armenian: Գրիգոր Լուսաւորիչ translit. *Grigor Lusavorich*, Greek: *Γρηγόριος Φωστήρ* or *Φωτιστής*, *Gregorios Phoster* or *Photistes*) (c. 257 – c. 331) is the patron saint and first official head of the Armenian Apostolic Church. He was a religious leader who is credited with converting Armenia from paganism to Christianity, Armenia thus being the first nation to adopt Christianity as its official religion in 301 AD.

Beginnings

Gregory's father Anak, a Parthian, was charged with assassinating Khosrov I, one of the kings of the Arshakouni line, and was put to death. Gregory's mother was named Okohe. Gregory narrowly escaped execution with the help of Sopia and Yevtagh, his caretakers. Gregory was taken to Caesarea (present-day Kayseri) in Cappadocia where Sopia and Yevtagh hoped to raise him.

Gregory was given to the Christian Holy Father Phirmilianos (Euthalius) to be educated and was brought up as a devout Christian. He went on to marry Mariam, also a devout Christian; they had two sons, the younger of whom, Aristaces (Aristakes), succeeded his father.

At that time Tiridates III (Trdat the Great), a son of King Khosrau II, reigned. Influenced partly by the fact that Gregory was the son of his father's enemy, he ordered Gregory imprisoned for twelve (some sources indicate fourteen) years in a pit on the Ararat Plain under the present day church of Khor Virap located near the historical city Artashat in Armenia.

Gregory was eventually called forth from his pit in 297 to restore to sanity Tiridates III (a.k.a. Trdat), who had lost all reason after he was betrayed by Diocletian.

Diocletian invaded and vast amounts of territory from western provinces of Greater Armenia became "protectorates" of Rome.

Declaration of Christianity in Armenia

In 301 Gregory baptized Trdat (now known as Trdat the Great) along with members of the royal court and upper class as Christians. Trdat issued a decree by which he granted Gregory full rights to begin carrying out the conversion of the entire nation to the Christian faith. The same year Armenia became the first country to adopt Christianity as its state religion.

The newly built cathedral, the Mother Church in Echmiadzin became and remains the spiritual and cultural center of Armenian Christianity and center of the Armenian Apostolic Church. Most Armenians were baptized in Aratsani (upper Euphrates) and Yeraskh (Arax) rivers.

Many of the pre-Christian, traditional Indo-European, festivals and celebrations such as Tyarndarach (Trndez - associated with fire worship) and Vartavar (Vadarvar - associated with water worship), that dated back to thousands of years were preserved and continued in the form of Christian celebrations and chants.

In 302, Gregory received consecration as Patriarch of Armenia from Leontius of Caesarea, his childhood friend.

Retirement and Death

In AD 318, St. Gregory appointed his son Aristaces (Aristakes) as the next Catholicos in line of Armenia's Holy Apostolic Church to stabilize and continue strengthening Christianity not only in Armenia, but also in the Caucasus and Anatolia.

Gregory also placed and instructed his grandson Grigoris (Aristakes' son) in charge of the holy missions to the peoples and tribes of all of the Caucasus and Caucasian Albania. Grigoris was martyred by a fanatical mob, while preaching in Albania.

In his later years, Gregory withdrew to a small sanctuary near Mount Sebuh (Mt. Sepuh) in the Daranalia province (Manyats Ayr, Upper Armenia) with a small convent of monks, where he remained until his death.

Veneration

After his death his corpse was removed to the village of Thodanum (T'ordan -

modern Doğanköy, near Erzincan). His remains were scattered far and near in the reign of Zeno.

His head is believed to be now in Italy, his left hand at Echmiadzin in Armenia, and his right at the Holy See of Cilicia in Antelias, Lebanon.

In the eighth century, the iconoclast decrees in Greece caused a number of religious orders to flee the Byzantine Empire and seek refuge elsewhere.

San Gregorio Armeno in Naples was built in that century over the remains of a Roman temple dedicated to Ceres, by a group of nuns escaping from the Byzantine Empire with the relics of Gregory the Illuminator.

A number of prayers, and about thirty of the canons of the Armenian Church are ascribed to Gregory the Illuminator. The homilies appeared for the first time in a work called *Haschacnapadum* at Constantinople in 1737; a century afterwards a Greek translation was published at Venice by the Mekhiterists; and they have since been edited in German by J. M. Schmid (Ratisbon, 1872). The original authorities for Gregory's life are Agathangelos, whose *History of Tiridates* was published by the Mekhitarists in 1835; Moses of Chorene, *Historiae Armenicae*; and Simeon Metaphrastes.

A *Life of Gregory* by the Vartabed Matthew was published in the Armenian language at Venice in 1749 and was translated into English by the Rev. Father Malan (1868).

Gregory is honored with a feast day on the liturgical calendar of the Episcopal Church (USA) on March 23.

Gallery

Painting at the Holy See of Cilicia

Mosaic icon of St. Gregory the Illuminator, 14th century (Pammakaristos Church, Istanbul).

The Right Hand of Gregory the Illuminator in the museum of the Holy See of Cilicia at Antelias, Lebanon

Saint Gregory the Illuminator Cathedral, Yerevan, (finished in 2001) contains the remains of St Gregory

Gregory the Illuminator illustration in 1898 book «Illustrated Armenia and Armenians»

Source (edited): "http://en.wikipedia.org/wiki/Gregory_the_Illuminator"

Hovhannes Draskhanakerttsi

Hovhannes Draskhanakerttsi (Հովհաննէս Դրասխանակերտցի, John of Drasxanakert, i.e. Gyumri, various spellings) was Catholicos of Armenia from 897 to 925, and a noted chronicler and historian. He is called **John V the Historian**, and is known for his *History of Armenia*. It was printed at the end of the seventeenth century. There is a recent English translation (1987) by Krikor Maksoudian. After returning the Catholicosate to Dvin since it had been reclaimed from the Arabs, he moved it again to Vaspurakan around 924. According to local traditions, Hovhannes was buried in Vaspurakan at either Joroy Vank or in the monastery of Akhtamar.

Source (edited): "http://en.wikipedia.org/wiki/Hovhannes_Draskhanakerttsi"

Isaac of Armenia

Saint Isaac

Isaac or **Sahak of Armenia** (338–439) was Catholicos (or Patriarch) of Armenia. He is sometimes known as "Isaac the Great," and as "Սահակ Պարթև / Sahak Parthev" in Armenian, owing to his Parthian origin.

Isaac was son of the Christian Saint Narses and descended from the family of Saint Gregory the Illuminator. He was the fifth catholicos of the Arsacid Dynasty of Armenia after St. Gregory I the Enlightener (301–325), St. Aristaces I (325–333), St. Vrtanes I (333–341) and St. Husik I (341–347).

Catholicos Sahak Partev, by Francesco Maggiotto

Left an orphan at a very early age, he received an excellent literary education in Constantinople, particularly in the Eastern languages. After his election as patriarch he devoted himself to the religious and scientific training of his people. Armenia was then passing through a grave crisis. In 387 it had lost its independence and been divided between the Byzantine Empire and Persia; each division had at its head an Armenian but feudatory king. In the Byzantine territory, however, the Armenians were forbidden the use of the Syriac language, until then exclusively used in divine worship: for this the Greek language was to be substituted, and the country gradually hellenized; in the Persian districts, on the contrary, Greek was absolutely prohibited, while Syriac was greatly favoured. In this way the ancient culture of the Armenians was in danger of disappearing and national unity was seriously compromised.

To save both Isaac invented, with the aid of Saint Mesrob, the Armenian alphabet and began to translate the Christian Bible; their translation from the Syriac Peshito was revised by means of the Septuagint, and even, it seems, from the Hebrew text (between 410 and 430). The liturgy also, hitherto Syrian was translated into Armenian, drawing at the same time on the liturgy of Saint Basil of Caesarea, so as to obtain for the new service a national colour. Isaac had already established schools for higher education with the aid of disciples whom he had sent to study at Edessa, Melitene, Constantinople, and elsewhere. Through them he now had the principal masterpieces of Greek and Syrian Christian literature translated, e.g. the writings of Athanasius, Cyril of Jerusalem, Basil, the two Gregorys (Gregory of Nazianzus and Gregory of Nyssa), John Chrysostom, Ephrem the Syrian, etc. Armenian literature in its golden age was, therefore, mainly a borrowed literature.

Through Isaac's efforts the churches and monasteries destroyed by the Persians were rebuilt, education was cared for in a generous way, Zoroastrianism which Shah Yazdegerd I tried to set up was cast out, and three councils held to re-establish ecclesiastical discipline. Isaac is said to have been the author of liturgical hymns.

Two letters, written by him to Theodosius II and to Atticus of Constantinople, have been preserved. A third letter addressed to Saint Proclus of Constantinople was not written by him, but dates from the tenth century. Neither did he have any share, as was wrongly ascribed to him, in the First Council of Ephesus of 431, though, in consequence of disputes which arose in Armenia between the followers of Nestorius and the disciples of Acacius of Melitene and Rabbula, Isaac and his church did appeal to Constantinople and through Saint Proclus obtained the desired explanations.

A man of enlightened piety and of very austere life, Isaac owed his deposition by the king in 426 to his great independence of character. In 430, he was allowed to resume his patriarchal throne. In his extreme old age he seems to have withdrawn into solitude, dying at the age of 110. The precise date of his death is not known, but it seems to have occurred between 439 and 441. Hovhannes Draskhanakerttsi says his body was taken to Taron and buried in the village of Ashtishat. Several days are consecrated to his memory in the Armenian Apostolic Church.

Source (edited): "http://en.wikipedia.org/wiki/Isaac_of_Armenia"

Jude the Apostle

Jude was one of the Twelve Apostles of Jesus. He is generally identified with **Thaddeus**, and is also variously called **Jude of James**, **Jude Thaddaeus**, **Judas Thaddaeus** or **Lebbaeus**. He is sometimes identified with Jude, "brother of Jesus", but is clearly distinguished from Judas Iscariot, another disciple and later the betrayer of Jesus.

The Armenian Apostolic Church honors Thaddeus along with Saint Bartholomew as its patron saints. In the Roman Catholic Church he is the patron saint of desperate cases and lost causes.

Saint Jude's attribute is a club. He is also often shown in icons with a flame around his head. This represents his presence at Pentecost, when he received the Holy Spirit with the other apostles. Another common attribute is Jude holding an image of Jesus Christ, in the image of Edessa. In some instances he may be shown with a scroll or a book (the Epistle of Jude) or holding a carpenter's rule.

Identity

St. Thaddeus, St. Sandukht and other Christians in Sanatruk's prison

Symbol of his martyrdom

Monastery in Iran

Church of Saints Simon and Jude Thaddeus in Rudno, Poland.

Procession in Lima, Peru.

New Testament

Jude is clearly distinguished from Judas Iscariot, another disciple and later the betrayer of Jesus. Both "Jude" and "Judas" are translations of the name Ἰούδας in the Greek original New Testament, which in turn is a Greek variant of Judah, a name which was common among Jews at the time. In most bibles in languages other than English and French, Jude and Judas are referred to by the same name.

"Jude of James" is only mentioned twice in the New Testament: in the lists of apostles in Luke 6:16 and Acts 1:13.

The name by which Luke calls the Apostle, "Jude of James" is ambiguous as to the relationship of Jude to this James. Though such a construction sometimes connotated a relationship of father and son, it has been traditionally interpreted as "Jude, brother of James" (Luke 6:16) though Protestants (for instance, the New International Version translation) usually identify him as "Jude son of James".

The Gospel of John also once mentions a disciple called "Judas not Iscariot" (John 14:22). This is often accepted to be the same person as the apostle Jude, though some scholars see the identification as uncertain.

In some Latin manuscripts of Matthew 10:3, he is called Judas the Zealot.

Possible Identity with Thaddeus

In the comparable apostle-lists of Matthew 10:3 and Mark 3:18, Jude is omitted, but there is a Thaddeus (or in some manuscripts of Matthew 10:3, "Lebbaeus who was surnamed Thaddaeus") listed in his place. This has led many Christians since early times to harmonize the lists by positing a "Jude Thaddeus", known by either name. This is made plausible by the fact that "Thaddeus" seems to be a nickname (see Thaddeus).

A further complication is the fact that the name "Judas" was tarnished by Judas Iscariot. It has been argued that for this reason it is unsurprising that Mark and Matthew refer to him by an alternate name.

Some Biblical scholars reject this theory, however, holding that Jude and Thaddeus did not represent the same person. Scholars have proposed alternate theories to explain the discrepancy: an unrecorded replacement of one for the other during the ministry of Jesus because of apostasy or death; the possibility that "twelve" was a symbolic number and an estimation; or simply that the names were not recorded perfectly by the early church.

Thaddeus the apostle is generally seen as a different person from Thaddeus of Edessa, one of the Seventy Disciples.

Brother of Jesus?

Opinion is divided on whether Jude the apostle is the same as Jude, brother of Jesus, who is mentioned in Mark 6:3 and Matthew 13:55-57, and is the traditional author of the Epistle of Jude.

Some Catholics believe the two Judes are the same person, while Protestants do not.

Tradition and legend

Tradition holds that Saint Jude preached the Gospel in Judea, Samaria, Idumaea, Syria, Mesopotamia and Libya. He is also said to have visited Beirut and Edessa, though the emissary of latter mission is also identified as Thaddeus of Edessa, one of the Seventy. The 14th century writer Nicephorus Callistus makes Jude the bridegroom at the wedding at Cana.

The legend reports that St. Jude was born into a Jewish family in Paneas, a town in Galilee later rebuilt by the Romans and renamed Caesarea Philippi. In all probability he spoke both Greek and Aramaic, like almost all of his contemporaries in that area, and was a farmer by trade. According to the legend, St. Jude was a son of Clopas and his wife Mary, a sister of the Virgin Mary. Tradition has it that Jude's father, Clopas, was murdered because of his forthright and outspoken devotion to the risen Christ. After Mary's death, miracles were attributed to her intercession.

Although Saint Gregory the Illuminator is credited as the "Apostle to the Armenians", when he baptized King Tiridates III of Armenia in 301, converting the Armenians, the Apostles Jude and Bartholomew are traditionally believed to have been the first to bring Christianity to Armenia, and are therefore venerated as the patron saints of the Armenian Apostolic Church. Linked to this tradition is the Saint Thaddeus Monastery (now in Northern Iran) and Saint Bartholomew Monastery (now in southeastern Turkey) which were both constructed in what was then Armenia.

Death and remains

According to the Armenian tradition, Saint Jude suffered martyrdom about 65 AD in Beirut, in the Roman province of Syria, together with the apostle Simon the Zealot, with whom he is usually connected. Their acts and martyrdom were recorded in an *Acts of Simon and Jude* that was among the collection of passions and legends traditionally associated with the legendary Abdias, bishop of Babylon, and said to have been translated into Latin by his disciple Tropaeus Africanus, according to the *Golden Legend* account of the saints. Saints Simon and Jude are venerated together in the Roman Catholic Church on October 28.

Sometime after his death, Saint Jude's body was brought from Beirut to Rome and placed in a crypt in St. Peter's Basilica which is visited by many devotees. According to popular tradition, the remains of St. Jude were preserved in an Armenian monastery on an island in the northern part of Issyk-Kul Lake in Kyrgyzstan at least until the mid-15th century. Later legends either deny that the remains are preserved there or claim that they were moved to a yet more desolate stronghold in the Pamir Mountains. Recent discovery of the ruins of what could be that monastery may put an end to the dispute.

Iconography

Jude is traditionally depicted carrying the image of Jesus in his hand or close to his chest, betokening the legend of the Image of Edessa, recorded in apocryphal correspondence between Jesus and Abgar which is reproduced in Eusebius' *History Ecclesiastica, I, xiii*. Eusebius relates that King Abgar of Edessa (now Şanlıurfa in southeast Turkey) sent a letter to Jesus seeking a cure for an illness afflicting him. With the letter he sent his envoy *Hannan*, the keeper of the archives, offering his own home city to Jesus as a safe dwelling place. The envoy painted a likeness of Jesus with choice paints (or alternatively, impressed with Abgar's faith, Jesus pressed his face into a cloth and gave it to *Hannan*) to take to Abgar with his answer. Upon seeing Jesus' image, the king placed it with great honor in one of his palatial houses. After Christ's execution, Thomas the Apostle sent Jude to King Abgar and the king was cured. Astonished, he converted to Christianity, along with many of the people under his rule. Additionally, St. Jude is often depicted with a flame above his head, representing his presence at Pentecost, when he was said to have received the Holy Spirit with the other apostles.

Veneration

The Order of Preachers (the Dominicans) began working in present day Armenia soon after their founding in 1216. There was a substantial devotion to St. Jude in this area at that time, by both Roman Catholic and Orthodox Christians. This lasted until persecution drove Christians from the area in the 18th century. Devotion to Saint Jude began again in earnest in the 19th century, starting in Italy and Spain, spreading to South America, and finally to the U.S. (starting in the area around Chicago) owing to the influence of the Claretians and the Dominicans in the 1920s.

Saint Jude is the patron saint of the Chicago Police Department and of Clube de Regatas do Flamengo (a soccer team in Rio de Janeiro, Brazil). His other patronages include desperate situations and hospitals. One of his namesakes is St. Jude Children's Research Hospital in Memphis, Tennessee, which has helped many children with terminal illnesses and their families since its founding in 1962. His feast day is October 28 (Roman Catholic Church, the Anglican Communion and Lutheran Church) and June 19 (Eastern Orthodox Church).

A common Roman Catholic prayer is:

" *O most holy apostle, Saint Jude, faithful servant and friend of Jesus, the Church honoureth and invoketh thee universally, as the patron of hopeless cases, and of things almost despaired of. Pray for me, who am so miserable. Make use, I implore thee, of that particular privilege accorded to thee, to bring visible and speedy help where help was almost despaired of. Come to mine assistance in this great need, that I may receive the consolation and succor of Heaven in all my necessities, tribulations, and sufferings, particularly (here make your request) and that I may praise God with thee and all the elect throughout eternity. I promise thee, O blessed Jude, to be ever mindful of this great favour, to always honour thee as my special and powerful patron, and to gratefully encourage devotion to thee. Amen.* "

An alternative prayer:

" *May the Sacred Heart of Jesus be adored, glorified, loved and preserved now and forever. Sacred Heart of Jesus have mercy on us, Saint Jude worker of Miracles, pray for us, Saint Jude helper and keeper of the hopeless, pray for us, Thank you Saint Jude.* "

In some daily newspapers people will place classified ads seeking the aid of St. Jude or thanking him for his intercession.

Shrines

U.S.A.
- National Shrine of St. Jude, Chicago, IL
- Dominican Shrine of St. Jude, Chicago, IL
- Nationwide Center of St. Jude Devotions, Baltimore, MD
- Dominican Monastery of Saint Jude in Marbury, AL
- St. Jude Maronite Catholic Church in Orlando, FL
- Shrine Church of St. Jude, Brooklyn, New York

Australia
- St Jude's Catholic Church, Langwarrin, VIC, Australia

India
- St Jude's Shrine, Jhansi-284 001, India
- St. Jude's Shrine, Yoodhapuram, Angamaly, Kerala, India
- St. Jude's Church, Ettekkar, Aluva, Kerala, India
- St. Jude Pilgrim Shrine, Killippalam, Trivandrum, Kerala, India
- St. Jude Shrine, Koothattukulam, Kerala, India
- St. Joseph's Church, Thevara, Kerala, India
- St. Jude Shrine, Kureekad, Chottanikkara, Kerala, India
- St. Jude Shrine, Maruthimoodu, Pathanapuram Road, Adoor, Pathanamthitta District, Kerala

Sri Lanka
- St Jude's Church Indigolla, Gampaha, Sri Lanka

Source (edited): "http://en.wikipedia.org/wiki/Jude_the_Apostle"

Karekin I

Karekin I (Eastern Armenian pronunciation: Garegin I) (Armenian: Գարեգին Ա. Սարգիսյան) (August 27, 1932 - June 29, 1999), served as the Catholicos of the Armenian Apostolic Church between 1995 and 1999. Previously, he served as the Catholicos of Cilicia from 1983 to 1994 under the name Karekin II (Armenian: Գարեգին Բ. Սարգիսյան).

Beginnings

Karekin, baptized Neshan Sarkissian, was born in Kesab, Syria, where he attended the Armenian elementary school. In 1946 he was admitted to the Theological Seminary of the Armenian Catholicate of Cilicia and in 1949 ordained a deacon. In 1952, after having graduated with high honors, he was ordained a celibate priest and renamed Karekin. He joined the order of the Armenian Catholicosate of Cilicia.

In 1955 he presented his doctoral thesis on the subject "The Theology of the Armenian Church, According to Liturgical Hymns Sharakans" and was promoted to the ecclesiastical degree of Vardapet. In next year he served as member of the faculty of the theological seminary in Antelias, Lebanon. He studied theology for two years at Oxford University and wrote *The Council of Chalcedon and the Armenian Church*, published in 1965 in London. Upon his return to Lebanon, he served as dean of the seminary.

From 1963, he became an aide to Catholicos Khoren I in which function he had many ecumenical contacts. He served as observer at the Second Vatican Council, the Lambeth Conference of 1968 and the Addis Ababa Conference of the heads of the Oriental Orthodox Churches. He lectured on theology, literature, history and culture at universities in Beirut, Romania, Moscow and Kotayyam (India).

His ecclesiastical career advanced quickly: In 1963 he was elevated to senior archmandrite and on January 19, 1964, consecrated bishop by Catholicos Khoren.

In 1971 he was elected Prelate of the Diocese of New Julfa in Isfahan, Iran.

In 1973, he received the rank of archbishop and was appointed Pontifical Legate of the Eastern Prelacy of the Armenia's Holy Apostolic Church of America (in New York) and in 1975 its Primate.

During his time in the United States, he took special care of the younger generation of Armenians and played a key role in the fundraising for Lebanon 1976-1977.

Catholicos Coadjutor of the Holy

See of Cilicia (1977-1983)

In 1977, he was elected Catholicos of the Catholicosate of Cilicia and served as Catholicos Coadjutor (Armenian: Աթոռակից Կաթողիկոս) until the death of Catholicos Khoren I in 1983.

Catholicos of the Holy See of Cilicia (1983-1994)

When fully installed as Catholicos of the Great House of Cilicia, Karekin lavished special attention on religious education, modernizing and promoting the theological seminary. His pontifical visits took him to Lebanon, Syria, Iran, Cyprus, the United States and Canada, as well as Kuwait and the other Arab states of the Persian Gulf.

Another important facet of his Catholicosate were his ecumenical contacts. Karekin undertook ecumenical visits to Pope John Paul II, Robert Runcie, the Archbishop of Canterbury, and Shenouda III, Pope of the Coptic Church, but also to the Swiss Reformed Churches and the Lutheran Churches of Denmark and Germany. In 1989 he was elected honorary president of the Middle East Council of Churches.

Karekin wrote several books and booklets in Armenian, English, and French and published many articles and studies on theological, Armenological, philosophical, ethical and literary subjects in periodicals.

He also made frequent visits to the Mother See of the Apostolic Church and expressed solidarity on a visit of the earthquake area in Armenia 1988 together with Catholicos Vazgen I.

Catholicos of All Armenians, Mother See of Holy Etchmiadzin (1994-1999)

The tomb of Karekin I at the Mother See of Holy Etchmiadzin.

After the death of Catholicos Vazgen I in 1994, Catholicos Karekin Sarkissian was elected Supreme Patriarch and Catholicos of All Armenians by a National Ecclesiastical Assembly of 400 delegates and hereafter became known as Karekin I, being the first Supreme Patriarch with that name.

In November 1998, Karekin I underwent cancer treatment in New York. He appointed archbishop Karekin Nersessian, the later Karekin II, as Vicar General. Karekin I died in June 1999.

Source (edited): "http://en.wikipedia.org/wiki/Karekin_I"

Karekin II

Catholicos Karekin II (Armenian: Գարեգին Բ) is the current head of the Holy Armenian Apostolic Church.

He was born as Ktrij Nersessian in Voskehat, Armenia, on August 21, 1951. He entered the Gevorkian Theological Seminary at Echmiadzin in 1965 and graduated with honors in 1971. He was ordained to the diaconate deacon in 1970. Later he became a monk and was ordained a celibate priest in 1972. In the late 1970s the Catholicos of that period encouraged him to study outside of Armenia. This led to him continuing his studies in Vienna, Bonn University, and Zagorsk, Russia. On October 23, 1983, he was consecrated bishop at Echmiadzin. He became an archbishop in 1992.

In 1988, he took an active role in helping his people overcome the Armenian earthquake. He has built a number of churches and schools. He also showed an interest in using modern technology and telecommunications to help the life of his churches as well as dealing with the legacies of the Soviet era.

In 1999, he was elected Catholicos of All Armenians at the Mother See of Holy Etchmiadzin, succeeding His Holiness, Karekin I. His relations with Pope John Paul II were generally positive. When the Pope visited Armenia in 2001, he stayed with the Catholicos.

In 2006, Karekin made a weeklong visit to Istanbul, Turkey, to meet with Ecumenical Patriarch Bartholomew I and to bless the city's Armenian community. During his visit he caused some controversy by affirming the Armenian Genocide, which Turkey vehemently denies, and insisting on its recognition.

In October 2007, he began a second visit to the United States.

On October 10, 2007, he offered the opening prayer for the day's session of the United States House of Representatives.

His ecumenical trip to India to meet Baselios Thoma Didymos I, Catholicos of the East in November 2008, has strengthened the communion of Armenian and Indian Orthodox Churches.

Source (edited): "http://en.wikipedia.org/wiki/Karekin_II"

Khachig I of Armenia

Catholicos Khachig I (Armenian: Խաչիկ Ա. Արշարունի) was the Catholicos of the Armenian Apostolic Church between 973 and 992.

After a one year vacancy due to a confusing period where there were two rival Catholicoi, King Ashot III "the Merciful" called an assembly to pick a new Catholicos. Khachik, a relative of the Catholicos Ananias was selected and was able to settle the problems which had arisen from the dueling Catholicoi and the schism it caused.

Source (edited): "http://en.wikipedia.org/wiki/Khachig_I_of_Armenia"

Khoren I

Khoren I Mesrop Paroyan (Armenian: Խորեն Ա. Բարոյան) (24 November 1914, Nicosia - 9 February 1983, Antelias) was the Catholicos of the Holy See of Cilicia, from 1963 to 1983.

He was preceded by Zareh I. Because of poor health Karekin II (Cilicia) was elected as Catholicos Coadjutor in 1977, a post he served assisting Catholicos Khoren I until the latter's death, when Karekin succeeded him as Karekin II of Cilicia.

Source (edited): "http://en.wikipedia.org/wiki/Khoren_I"

Khoren I of Armenia

Khoren I of Armenia was the Catholicos of the Armenian Apostolic Church from 1932–1938.

Tombstone of Khoren I, Catholicos of All Armenians, at Mother Cathedral of Holy Etchmiadzin

Khoren I is buried near the Mother Cathedral of Holy Etchmiadzin. After his death, the position remained vacant for 7 years (1938–1945) before the election of Catholicos George VI of Armenia.

Source (edited): "http://en.wikipedia.org/wiki/Khoren_I_of_Armenia"

Lazar I of Armenia

Catholicos Lazar I of Armenia was the Catholicos of the Armenian Apostolic Church between 1737 and 1751. He is notable for the numerous troubles he personally got into during his reign.

Lazar had been bishop of Smyrna, Turkey and was a native of Jahuk. He was said to be extremely beloved by his nation and many wanted him to be the Catholicos when Abraham III died, though another party supported Gregory the Armenian Patriarch of Jerusalem. Lazar's supporters were more numerous and upon his election Lazar left Smyrna and made a grand procession to Erzurum, where the bishop received him. The governor there however detained him for a time until suddenly dying, an event blamed on divine wrath directed by Lazar. Lazar in turn blamed the bishop and was allowed to leave, escaping to Kars. Meanwhile word arrived in Erzurum that the sultan demanded Lazar's arrest as he had not applied to the sultan for proper approval of letters patent for his election. Lazar was notified of the danger and he fled to Persia before making it to Etchmiadzin. A few years later Lazar came into conflict with the prince of Persia and was almost executed for it but escaped by paying a large fine. Another time, the Persian vizier who also did not like Lazar convinced the shah that Lazar was a problem. The shah summoned Lazar to see him and grew very angry at him, having the Catholicos's grand tent destroyed. He had Lazar dragged before him and to be beaten severely. He was led to prison and kept for five months until he paid the required fine. Sometime after his return, Lazar had a rival monk Peter Kytheur persecuted and tortured, until he was finally able to leave for refuge in Karin. From there the monk wrote about his torture to many Armenian churches and many people began to complain about Lazar. The governor of Erevan was asked to intervene and so he gathered the Armenian clergy and asked them to decide on the matter. The clergy said they did not want Lazar, so he was arrested and taken to Sevanavank. Peter Kytheur was anointed the new Catholicos in his place, who then excommunicated Lazar. Lazar had a group of supporters who agitated for his release, and around this time Ebrahim Afshar became the new shah of Persian. Lazar's supporters got the shah to have Lazar released from prison and not long after (some say thanks to bribes to the shah) he had Lazar restored as Catholicos. Peter Kytheur was fettered and thrown in a dungeon where he eventually died of starvation after being Catholicos for ten months, though his name is not included on the Wikipedia official list. Lazar died three years after his restoration.

Source (edited): "http://en.wikipedia.org/wiki/Lazar_I_of_Armenia"

List of Catholicoi of Armenia

This is a list of The **Catholicoi of all Armenians**, head bishops of the Armenian Apostolic Church.

Catholicoi of Armenia

(Name in English, dates, Armenian name in Eastern Armenian spelling)

Apostolic Era

- St. Thaddeus the Apostle (43-66) -- Սբ. Թադեոս Առաքյալ
- St. Bartholomew the Apostle (60-68) -- Սբ. Բարդուղիմէոս Առաքյալ
- St. Zacharias (68-72) -- Սբ. Զաքարիա
- St. Zementus (72-76) -- Սբ. Զեմենդոս
- St. Atrnerseh (77-92) -- Սբ. Ատրներսեհ
- St. Mushe (93-123) -- Սբ. Մուշե
- St. Shahen (124-150) -- Սբ. Շահեն
- St. Shavarsh 151-171—Սբ. Շավարշ
- St. Leontius (172-190) -- Սբ. Ղեոնդիոս

Sophene Era

- St. Merozanes (240-270) -- Սբ. Մերուժան
- St. Gregory I the Illuminator (288-325) -- Սուրբ Գրիգոր Ա. Պարթև (Լուսավորիչ)

First Echmiadzin era 301-452

Arsacid Dynasty (from 301 to 428 the episcopal office is hereditary)

- St. Gregory I the Illuminator (301-325) -- Սուրբ Գրիգոր Ա. Պարթև (Լուսավորիչ)
- St. Aristaces I (325-333) -- Սբ. Արիստակես Ա. Պարթև
- St. Vrtanes I (333-341) -- Սբ. Վրթանես Ա. Պարթև
- St. Husik I (341-347) -- Սբ. Հուսիկ Ա. Պարթև

Syrians descent

- Daniel I of Armenia (347) -- Դանիել Ա.

Ashishatts Dynasty

- Pharen I of Armenia (348-352) -- Փառեն Ա. Աշտիշատցի

Arsacid Dynasty

- St. Nerses I the Great (353-373) -- Սուրբ Ներսես Ա. Մեծ (Պարթև)

Albaniosid Dynasty

- Sahak I (373-377) -- Սահակ Ա. Մանազկերտցի
- Zaven I (377-381) -- Զավեն Ա. Մանազկերտցի
- Aspuraces I (381-386) -- Ասպուրակես Ա. Մանազկերտցի

Arsacid Dynasty

- St. Sahak I (387-428) -- Սբ. Սահակ Ա. Պարթև

Syrians descent

- Brkisho of Armenia (428-432) -- Բրկիշո
- Samuel of Armenia (432-437) -- Սամվել

Non-Hereditary Bishop

- St. Hovsep I (437-452) -- Սբ. Հովսեփ Ա. Հողոցմեցի

Dvin era 452-927

- Melitus I (452-456) -- Մելիտե Ա. Մանազկերտցի
- Moses I (456-461) -- Մովսես Ա. Մանազկերտցի
- St. Kyud I (461-478) -- Սբ. Գյուտ Ա. Արահեզացի
- St. John I (478-490) -- Սբ. Հովհաննես Ա. Մանդակունի
- Babken I (490-516) -- Բաբկեն Ա. Որսնեցի
- Samuel I (516-526) -- Սամվել Ա. Արծկեցի
- Mushe I (526-534) -- Մուշե Ա. Այլաբերցի
- Sahak II (534-539) -- Սահակ Բ. Ուղկեցի
- Christopher I (539-545) -- Քրիստափոր Ա. Տիրառիջցի
- Ghevond I (545-548) -- Ղևոնդ Ա. Եռաստեցի
- Nerses II (548-557) --Ներսես Բ. Բագրևանցի
- John II (557-574)-- Հովհաննես Բ. Գաբեղենցի
- Moses II (574-604) -- Մովսես Բ. Եղիվարդեցի
  - vacant 604-607, administered by Verthanes Qerthol the Gramatic
- Abraham I (607-615) -- Աբրահամ Ա. Աղբաթանեցի
- Gomidas I (615-628) -- Կոմիտաս Ա. Աղցեցի
- Christopher II (628-630), died aft. 630—Քրիստափոր Բ. Ապահունի
- Ezra I (630-641) -- Եզր Ա. Փառաժնակերտցի
- Nerses III the Builder (641-661) --

Ներսես Գ. Տայեցի (Շինարար)
- Anastasius I (661-667) -- Անաստաս Ա. Ակոռեցի
- Israel I (667-677) -- Իսրայել Ա. Որմեցի
- Sahak III (677-703) -- Սահակ Գ. Ձորոփորեցի
- Elias I (703-717) -- Եղիա Ա. Արճիշեցի
- St. John III the Philosopher (717-728) -- Սբ. Հովհաննես Գ. Օձնեցի (Փիլիսոփա)
- David I (728-741) -- Դավիթ Ա. Արամոնեցի
- Dertad I (741-764) -- Տրդատ Ա. Որմեցի
- Dertad II (764-767) -- Տրդատ Բ. Դասնավորեցի
- Sion I (767-775) -- Սիոն Ա. Բավոնեցի
- Isaiah I (775-788) -- Եսայի Ա. Եղիպատրուշեցի
- Stephen I (788-790) -- Ստեփանոս Ա. Դվնեցի
- Joab I (790-791) -- Յովաբ Ա. Դվնեցի
- Solomon I (791-792) -- Սողոմոն Ա. Գառնեցի
- George I (792-795) -- Գևորգ Ա. Բյուրականցի
- Joseph I (795-806) -- Հովսեփ Բ. Փարպեցի
- David II (806-833) -- Դավիթ Բ. Կակաղեցի
- John IV (833-855) -- Հովհաննես Դ. Ավայեցի
- Zacharias I (855-876) -- Զաքարիա Ա. Ձագեցի
- George II (877-897) -- Գևորգ Բ. Գառնեցի
- Mashdotz I (897-898) -- Մաշտոց Ա. Եղվարդեցի

Aghtamar era 927-947
- John V the Historian (898-929) -- Հովհաննես Ե. Դրասխանակերտցի
- Stephen II (929-930) -- Ստեփանոս Բ. Ռշտունի
- Theodore I (930-941) -- Թեոդորոս Ա. Ռշտունի
- Yeghishe I (941-946) -- Եղիշե Ա. Ռշտունի

Arghina era 947-992
- Ananias I (949-968) -- Անանիա Ա. Մոկացի
- Vahan I (968-969) -- Վահան Ա. Սյունեցի
- Stephen III (969-972) -- Ստեփանոս Գ. Սևանցի
- Khachig I (973-992) -- Խաչիկ Ա. Արշարունի

Ani era 992-1058
- Sarkis I (992-1019), d. aft. 1019—Սարգիս Ա. Սևանցի
- Peter I (1019–1058) Պետրոս Ա. Գետադարձ

During this time the see was transferred to Cilicia, from 1058 till 1441 (see List of Armenian Catholicoi of Cilicia for continued succession).

Catholicoi of the Mother See of Holy Echmiadzin and All Armenians

Second Echmiadzin era 1441-present
- Giragos I (1441–1443) -- Կիրակոս Ա. Վիրապեցի
- Gregory X (1443–1465) -- Գրիգոր Ժ. Ջալալբեկյանց
  - Aristaces II (*Coadjutor*) (1465–1469) -- Արիստակես Բ. Ատրպատակալ
- Sarkis II the Relic-Carrier (1469–1474) -- Սարգիս Բ. Աջատառ
- John VII the Relic-Bearer (1474–1484), d. 1506—Հովհաննես Է. Աջակիր
- Sarkis III the Other (1484–1515) -- Սարգիս Գ. Մյուսայլ
- Zacharias II (1515–1520) -- Զաքարիա Բ. Վաղարշապատցի
- Sarkis IV (1520–1536) -- Սարգիս Դ. Վրաստանցի
- Gregory XI (1536–1545) -- Գրիգոր ԺԱ. Բյուզանդացի
- Stephen V (1545–1567) -- Ստեփանոս Ե. Սալմաստեցի
- Michael I (1567–1576) -- Միքայել Ա. Սեբաստացի
- Gregory XII (1576–1590) -- Գրիգոր ԺԲ. Վաղարշապատցի
- David IV (1590–1629), d. 1633—Դավիթ Դ. Վաղարշապատցի
- Moses III (1629–1632) -- Մովսես Գ. Տաթևացի
- Philip I (1633–1655) -- Փիլիպոս Ա. Աղբակեցի
- Jacob IV (1655–1680) -- Հակոբ Դ. Ջուղայեցի
- Eliazar I (1681–1691) -- Եղիազար Ա. Այնթափցի
- Nahabed I (1691–1705) -- Նահապետ Ա. Եդեսացի
- Alexander I (1706–1714) -- Ալեքսանդր Ա. Ջուղայեցի
- Asdvadzadur (1715–1725) -- Աստվածատուր Ա. Համադանցի
- Garabed II (1725–1729) -- Կարապետ Բ. Ուլնեցի
- Abraham II (1730–1734) -- Աբրահամ Բ. Խոշաբեցի
- Abraham III (1734–1737) -- Աբրահամ Գ. Կրետացի
- Lazar I (1737–1751) -- Ղազար Ա. Ջահկեցի
- Minas I (1751–1753) -- Մինաս Ա. Ակնեցի
- Alexander II (1753–1755) -- Ալեքսանդր Բ. Բյուզանդացի
  - Sahak V (elected but never consecrated) (1755) -- Սահակ Ե.
  - *vacant* (1755–1759)
- Jacob V (1759–1763) -- Հակոբ Ե. Շամախեցի
- Simeon I (1763–1780) -- Սիմոն Ա. Երևանցի
- Luke I (1780–1799) -- Ղուկաս Ա. Կարնեցի
  - Joseph II (elected but never consecrated) (1800), d. 1801—Հովսեփ Բ.
  - David V (1801–1807) -- Դավիթ Ե. Էնեգերցի (Ղորղանյան)
- Daniel II (1802–1808) -- Դանիել Բ. Սուրմառեցի
- Yeprem I (1809–1830), d. 1835—Եփրեմ Ա. Ձորագեղցի
- John VIII (1831–1842) -- Հովհաննես Ը Կարբեցի
- Nerses V (1843–1857) -- Ներսես Ե. Աշտարակեցի
- Matthew I (1858–1865) -- Մատթեոս Ա.Կոնստանդնուպոլսեցի (Չուհաճյան)
- George IV (1866–1882) -- Գևորգ Դ. Կոնստանդնուպոլսեցի (Քերեստեճյան)
  - *vacant* (1882–1885)
- Magar (1885–1891) -- Մակար Ա. Թեղուտցի
- Mkrtich I Khrimian (1892–1907) --

- Մկրտիչ Ա. Վանեցի (Խրիմյան Հայրիկ)
- Matthew II (1908–1910) -- Մատթէոս Բ. Կոնստանդնուպոլսեցի (Իզմիրլյան)
- George V (1911–1930) -- Գէորգ Ե. Սուրէնյանց (Տփղիսեցի)
  - vacant (1930–1932)
- Khoren I (1932–1938) -- Խորէն Ա. Մուրադբեկյան (Տփղիսեցի)
  - vacant (1938–1945)
- George VI (1945–1954) -- Գէորգ Զ. Չորեքչյան (Նորնախիջևանցի)
- Vazgen I (1955–1994) -- Վազգէն Ա. Պալճյան (Բուխարեստցի)
- Karekin I (1995–1999) -- Գարեգին Ա. Սարգիսյան (Բէսարցի)
- Karekin II (1999–Present) -- Գարեգին Բ. Ներսիսյան (Ոսկեհատցի)

Source (edited): "http://en.wikipedia.org/wiki/List_of_Catholicoi_of_Armenia"

Mashdotz I

Catholicos Mashdotz I was the Catholicos of the Armenian Apostolic Church between 897 and 898. He was a monk of Sevanavank monastery and regarded as a very holy man. While a monk, he was asked by sparapet Abas to assist in overthrowing the current Catholicos, George II, and was promised the Catholicosate throne in return. Mashdotz wrote a long letter in response, rejecting the offer to rebel against the Catholicos, and chided Abas for his attempt. The plot failed and Mashdotz continued to be respected for his piety. Hovhannes Draskhanakerttsi reports that Mashdotz refused to even maintain a diet of bread and water, only eating vegetables. Upon the death of George II, King Smbat I and his associates elected Mashdotz the new Catholicos as they were impressed with him. He was known as a holy man and excellent teacher, but died after seven months as Catholicos. The same historian Hovhannes Draskhanakerttsi was asked by the king to be his replacement.

Source (edited): "http://en.wikipedia.org/wiki/Mashdotz_I"

Mkrtich Khrimian

"Mkrtich Khrimian near Echmiadzin" Ivan Aivazovsky 1885

Mkrtich Khrimian (Armenian: Մկրտիչ Խրիմեան; April 4, 1820 – October 27, 1907), also known as **Khrimian Hayrik** (Armenian: Խրիմեան Հայրիկ), was an Armenian writer, newspaper editor, and political and religious leader. He served as the Armenian Patriarch of Constantinople (1869–1873), Prelate of Van (1880–1885) and Catholicos of All Armenians (1892–1907). He devoted his life to the betterment of the Armenian people, especially the peasantry in eastern Anatolia.

Khrimian was born in Van on April 4, 1820. After receiving his primary education, he studied Grabar or classical Armenian as well as Armenology.

Service in Van, 1854-1869

In 1854, he was ordained a priest and entered priesthood in the monastery of Aght'amar. Khrimian, a progressivist, was resented by his conservative brethren, so he left the monastery and gave himself to independent service. Elsewhere, his sermons won him public admiration and affection among Armenians. Khrimian was known to be an excellent orator, his speeches full of color and emotion. He established a printing press at Varagavank in Van, and thereafter launched *Artsiv Vaspourakan* (*Eagle of Vaspourakan*), which was the first periodical publication in Armenia.

Khrimian urged Armenian peasants to defend themselves against hostile Kurds. He was also successful in repealing illegal taxes imposed against Christian Armenians by the Ottoman government.

In 1855, Khrimyan launched "Artsui Vaspurakan", the first periodical publication in Armenia. Garegin Shrvandztyants and Arsen Tokhmakhyan also worked on this periodical together with other pupils of a school founded by Khrimyan.

In 1857 later Khrimyan became the head of Taron, the dean of Saint Karapet seminary.

Armenian Patriarch of Constantinople, 1869-1873

In 1869, Khrimyan was elected Patriarch of Constantinople. Five years later he resigned this position and began his struggle against darkness and injustice. Carrying out an ambitious plan to enlighten his people, Khrimyan was thwarted in his efforts by the antagonism of fellow clergy who presented numerous obstacles to his work.

In 1876, on occasion of fire and robbery of Van, Khrimyan wrote "Vangoyzh", an inspirational appeal for efficient measures instead of complaining of losses and difficulties., When the Russo-Turkish war broke out, he wrote "Haygoyzh". These two works were enough to proclaim him "Khorenatsi of the 19th century."* He also wrote "Heavenly Land", "A Grandfather and a Grandson" and others. Most of Khrimyan's work greatly influenced the character and social thought of the people of his time.

In 1876, Khrimyan published "His Time and Counsel" in which he expressed his thoughts and views of the constitution of the Ottoman Empire.

In 1878, Khrimyan headed the delegation to represent the will of Armenian people at the Berlin Conference. Upon his return he stated in an eloquent speech entitled, "The Paper Ladle," that the hopes of the Armenian people for self-determination were ignored by the European community of nations.

Prelate of Van, 1880-1885

In 1878, Khrimyan sent his aid to the starving population of Van and founded an orphanage. In 1878, He began to serve as the Prelate of Van whose seat was at Varagavank.

In 1885 Khrimyan Hayrik was recalled to Constantinople. Turkish authorities did not appreciate his activities.

Later he was sent to Jerusalem, which, in fact, was an exile.

Catholicos of All Armenians, Echmiadzin (1892-1907)

Tombstone of Mkrtich Khrimian beside the entrance to Echmiadzin Cathedral

In the eyes of native people the personality of Khrimyan rose instantly; therefore in 1892 Khrimyan Hayrik was unanimously elected Catholicos of All Armenians. He moved to the Mother See of Holy Echmiadzin as head of the Armenian Apostolic Church. Because of his fatherly love and dedication to the common people, Mkrtich Khrimian was affectionately called Khrimian "Hayrik", which means "father" in the Armenian language.

In 1903 the Czarist government of Imperial Russia ordered the confiscation of all Armenian ecclesiastical and educational properties. Khrimian, then acting Catholicos, waged a heroic struggle against the decision, which came to success in 1905 when the Czar published a decree reopening Armenian schools and returning church properties.

In 1907 Catholicos Khrimyan died leaving a grieving nation. Khrimyan's life was an outstanding and extraordinary example of a leader's dynamic accomplishment in drawing his people closer and closer to their native land and sense of nationhood, both physically and spiritually.

Source (edited): "http://en.wikipedia.org/wiki/Mkrtich_Khrimian"

Moses III of Armenia

Catholicos Moses III (also **Movses III**) of Tatev was the Catholicos of the Armenian Apostolic Church between 1629 and 1632.

He was a pioneer of the reform movement within the church and his work was carried on by his successors. He also obtained protection from the Shah of Persia against local Muslim chieftains.

Source (edited): "http://en.wikipedia.org/wiki/Moses_III_of_Armenia"

Nahabed I of Armenia

Catholicos Nahabed I of Edessa was the Catholicos of the Armenian Apostolic Church between 1691 and 1705.

He was a virtuous man of meek disposition. He made many improvements to Etchmiadzin during his reign and attempted to reunite his countrymen. He wrote to Pope Innocent XII professing submission to the Roman Catholic church, for which shortly after Nahabed was expelled from Etchmiadzin by a bishop. This Bishop Stephen planned a coup and deposed the Catholicos, putting himself on the throne and reigning for 10 months, at which point the Armenian clergy seized him and restored Nahabed. Stephen's reign is not recognized as a pontifical reign because it was never recognized by other branches of the church as rules dictated needed to be done. Pope Innocent responded to the letter in 1696 with the gift of a papal throne, which is still on display in Etchmiadzin today. Nahabed again wrote of his submission to Rome, a move which inflamed the Armenian Patriarch of Constantinople when he learned of these moves. Much turmoil followed there with the Patriachate being usurped multiple times and leading to a division in the people. When Nahabed died there was still much confusion and turmoil amongst the people and so the pontificate stayed vacant for more than a year until Alexander of Julfa was called to the throne by general consent.

Source (edited): "http://en.wikipedia.org/wiki/Nahabed_I_of_Armenia"

Nerses III the Builder

Nerses III the Builder (Armenian: Ներսես Գ Շինող) was the Catholicos of the Armenian Apostolic Church between 641 and 661. He was originally from the village of Ishkhan in Tayk. He ruled at a troubled time during which Armenia had to choose between their neighbors Byzantines and Persians along with their new conquerors the Arabs.

Catholicos Nerses III received the title of the Builder due to the grand construction works he undertook during his reign. The most important ones were the construction of a chapel over the pit of imprisonment of St. Gregory the Illuminator at Khor Virap (which was replaced a thousand years later by the current church) and the magnificent cathedral of Zvartnots. One tradition says he might have been buried on the northern side of the church.

Source (edited): "http://en.wikipedia.org/wiki/Nerses_III_the_Builder"

Nerses V

Nerses V (Armenian: Ներսես Ե Աշտարակեցի) (1770 - February 13, 1857), served as the Catholicos of the Armenian Apostolic Church between 1843 and 1857. Previously, he served as the leader of Diocese of Georgia from 1811 to 1830, the leader of the Diocese of Bessarabia and Nakhijevan from 1830 to 1843.

Tombstone of Nerses V near Mother Cathedral of Holy Etchmiadzin

Nerses V is buried near Mother Cathedral of Holy Etchmiadzin.

Source (edited): "http://en.wikipedia.org/wiki/Nerses_V"

Parsegh of Cilicia

Parsegh of Cilicia was the Catholicos of the Armenian Apostolic Church between 1105 and 1113 and was nephew of Gregory II.

As Catholicos Gregory II had moved to Tarsus, far from the center of Armenian civilization for the past many centuries, the eastern Armenians considered themselves without a pontiff. Gregory had previously visited Ani and set up his nephew Parsegh as bishop there, and so later they gained Gregory's sanction to elect Parsegh their pontiff. Around this time two other rivals named themselves pontiff of their own regions: Theodorus and one named Paul in Marash. There was much enmity between them and cause of much confusion amongst the people. Paul saw this and decided to relinquish his seat and retire to his convent, at which time the nation at large recognized Gregory II alone as pontiff, with Parsegh as his deputy. In 1087 Parsegh deposed Theodorus and settled at Edessa. In 1103, after many requests, Gregory II finally accepted the invitation of Basil the Sly to move his residence to Rapan, in the vicinity of the city of Cheson, to spend his last years. As he left his Tarsus monastery, he took with him wards Gregory III of Cilicia and Nerses IV the Graceful, in whom he recognized future greatness. He entrusted the two preteens to the care of his nephew and deputy Parsegh as well as to his host Basil the Sly, and stated that on his death Parsegh should be made Catholicos to then be followed by Gregory. Parsegh had his seat sometimes in the desert of Shughr and sometimes in the city of Edessa. He saw to the education of Gregory and Nerses and soon ordained Gregory a priest. During this period the Persians invaded Cilicia but were defeated by the forces of Basil the Sly. Two years later though Cilicia was once again invaded, this time by Scythians. In 1111 they turned their sights on the fortress of Zovk which belonged to Gregory and Nerses's father Apirat Pahlavi, grandson of Gregorius Magistratus, at which he was killed. Parsegh died in the desert red convent of Shugr after being pontiff for thirty-one year, eight of those as sole ruler of the Armenian Church. Based on Gregory II's wishes, Gregory the son of Apirat was elected Catholicos at there at the red convent, only twenty years old.

Source (edited): "http://en.wikipedia.org/wiki/Parsegh_of_Cilicia"

Peter I of Armenia

Catholicos Peter I Ketadarz (? - died 1058) (Armenian: Պետրոս Ա. Գետադարձ) was the Catholicos of the Armenian Apostolic Church between 1019 and 1058. He was the brother of a former Catholicos Khachig I. He was the author of several works of sermons, anthems, and elegies on early Christian martyrs.

He was surnamed Ketadarz because he was said to have miraculously turned the current of a river toward its source. In later years Peter moved to Sebastia but later returned to Ani, at which point he was viewed with suspicious due to his long time away. He was induced to retire to Vaspurakan and remained shut up in a convent for four years in the early 1030s. The king appointed Deoskoros, abbot of Sanahin, as the new pontiff but the bishops would not recognize his authority. Deoskoros named a number of people described by historian Michael Chamich as "low" and "vile" to the priesthood and reinstated bishops who had been expelled for vices. This caused great disorder within the church and the clergy declared the king and other supporters of Deoskoros as anathema. To avoid this the king sent for Catholicos Peter to restore him to the pontifical chair. Deoskoros and those he appointed were defrocked. In 1042 after an interregnum in Armenia an assembly of generals named Gagik II the new king who Peter crowned. Gagik was overthrown after three years by the Byzantines when they captured Ani. A new governor was sent to Ani form Greece and Catholicos Peter was exiled from the city. He was soon seized by order of the emperor and taken to Constantinople where Peter was given a residence to keep him away from Armenia. He was taken to Sebastia by one who had pledged to the emperor that the Catholicos would not escape and he lived there for five years in the convent of the Holy Cross. He was eventually able to return from Armenia and died at an advanced age after a reign of 40 years. His nephew was elected as Khachig II of Cilicia.

Source (edited): "http://en.wikipedia.org/wiki/Peter_I_of_Armenia"

Pharen I of Armenia

Pharen I of Armenia (Armenian: Փառէն Ա. Աշիշատցի) was Catholicos in Armenia's Holy Apostolic Church of the Ashishatts Dynasty. He reigned for 5 years from 348 to 352 and was succeeded by St. Nerses I the Great of the Arsacid Dynasty of Armenia

Source (edited): "http://en.wikipedia.org/wiki/Pharen_I_of_Armenia"

Sahak I

Not to be confused with St. Sahak.

Sahak I (Armenian: Սահակ Ա. Մանազկերցի) was a catholicos of the Armenian Apostolic Church. He succeeded Saint Nerses I the Great and reigned from 373 to 377 AD and first of three catholicoi from the Albaniosid Dynasty

Source (edited): "http://en.wikipedia.org/wiki/Sahak_I"

Sahak III

Sahak III, was the Catholicos of Armenia from 677 through 703. According to the historian Hovhannes Draskhanakerttsi Sahak III was alive in Damascus, where he had gone to discuss peace instead of making war, while a Muslim warrior Okbay was moving with his army through the area of Vanand when the people there massacred them. Okbay returned to the Caliph to raise a large army against Armenia and destroy its churches and kill the population. Sahak asked to be allowed to go to Okbay to dissuade him from doing so, but fell ill when he arrived in Kharan. He wrote a letter imploring Okbay to not carry out his plan. Before he died he asked to have the letter placed in his palm, so that when Okbay came to receive it he would be taking it from his dead hand and perhaps reconsider. It is said that when Okbay arrived Sahak's hand moved to extend the letter to Okbay, who was impressed and carried out Sahak's wishes and sent Sahak's body back to Armenia with a letter to its princes pardoning them. Armenia was

Sarkis II the Relic-Carrier

Sarkis II the Relic-Carrier was the Catholicos of Armenian Apostolic Church from 1469-1474.

Source (edited): "http://en.wikipedia.org/wiki/Sarkis_II_the_Relic-Carrier"

Sarkis I of Armenia

Catholicos Sarkis I (Armenian: Սարգիս Ա. Սևանցի) was the Catholicos of the Armenian Apostolic Church between 992 and 1019. He was said to be mild mannered and humble, so that even as leader of the church he lived simply like a hermit. A terrible earthquake struck the land around the fourth year of his reign. The dormant sect of anti-clerical Tondrakians was revived during Sarkis's reign and he condemned it as anathema. He died shortly after and was succeeded by Peter I of Armenia, brother of the previous Catholicos Khachig I.

Source (edited): "http://en.wikipedia.org/wiki/Sarkis_I_of_Armenia"

Seats of the Catholicos of Armenians

Seats of the Catholicos of Armenians is the list of the seats of the Catholicos of Armenians

Source (edited): "http://en.wikipedia.org/wiki/Seats_of_the_Catholicos_of_Armenians"

St. Aristaces I

St Aristaces (also known as Aristakes) (Armenian: Սբ. Արիստակես Ա. Պարթ) was assigned by St. Gregory I the Enlightener as the next Armenian Catholicos in line of Armenia's Holy Apostolic Church, to stabilize and continue strengthening Christianity not only in Armenia, but also in the Caucasus and Anatolia. At the time, the position was hereditary and assigned to the Parthian dynasty.

Gregory also placed and instructed his grandson Grigoris (Aristakes' son) in charge of the holy missions to the peoples and tribes of all of the Caucasus and Caucasian Albania. Grigoris was martyred by a fanatical mob, while preaching in Albania.

After the assignemnet of his son as Catholicos, and after reaching his late eighties St. Gregory I the Enlightener withdrew to a small sanctuary near Mount Sebuh (Mt. Sepuh) in the Daranalia province (Manyats Ayr, Upper Armenia) with a small convent of monks, where he remained until his death.

St Aristaces I ruled from 325 until 333AD.

Source (edited): "http://en.wikipedia.org/wiki/St._Aristaces_I"

St. Husik

Saint Husik was Patriarch of Armenia and a martyr. According to P'awstos he was raised in the court of King Tiran of Armenia and married the daughter of Tiran when quite young. P'awstos goes as far as to say that Husik only coupled with his wife once, from which union were born two sons.

He was willing to denounce the evils of the king and his courtiers. At one point he went as far as to try and ban the king and his associates from the church at the time of a festival. For this he was martyred by being clubbed to death.

Source (edited): "http://en.wikipedia.org/wiki/St._Husik"

St. Husik I

St. Husik (Armenian: Սբ. Հուսիկ Ա. Պարթ) was Armenian Catholicos in Armenia's Holy Apostolic Church and fourth in line of then hereditary line of Parthian catholicoi, immediately after St. Gregory I the Enlightener, his son St. Aristaces I and St. Vrtanes I. He reigned from 341 to 347 AD.

Source (edited): "http://en.wikipedia.org/wiki/St._Husik_I"

St. Nerses I

Saint **Nerses I the Great** (Armenian: Սուրբ Ներսես Ա. Մեծ) was an Armenian Catholicos (or Patriarch) who lived in the fourth century. He was the father of another catholicos, Saint Sahak I. His father was At'anagenes and his mother was Bambish, the sister of King Tiran.

Born of the royal Gregorid stock, he spent his youth in Caesarea where he married Sanducht, a Mamikonian princess. After the death of his wife, he was appointed sword-bearer to King Arshak II. A few years later, having entered the ecclesiastical state, he was elected catholicos in 353.

His patriarchate marks a new era in Armenian history. Till then the Church had been more or less identified with the royal family and the nobles; Nerses brought it into closer connection with the people. At the Council of Ashtishat he promulgated numerous laws on marriage, fast days, and divine worship. He built schools and hospitals, and sent monks throughout the land to preach the Gospel.

Nerses held a synod at Ashtishat that, among other things, forbade people to marry their first cousin and forbade mutilation and other extreme actions in mourning.

Some of these reforms drew upon him the king's displeasure, and he was exiled, supposedly to Edessa. It was probably at some point during the later part of Arshak's reign that Nerses went to Constantinople to ensure the emperor's support of Armenia against the Persians. According to P'awstos Buzandac'i's account Emperor Valens became outraged at Nerses condemning his following the teachings of Arius and sent Nerses into exile. While Nerses was in exile Xad was the leader of the church in Armenia.

Upon the accession of pro-Arian King Pap (369) he returned to his see. Pap proved a dissolute and unworthy ruler and Nerses forbade him entrance to the church. Under the pretence of seeking a reconciliation, Pap invited Nerses to his table and reportedly poisoned him in 373.

Source (edited): "http://en.wikipedia.org/wiki/St._Nerses_I"

St. Vrtanes I

St Vrtanes (Armenian: Սբ. Վրթանես Ա. Պարթև) was Armenian Catholicos in Armenia's Holy Apostolic Church immediately after St. Gregory I the Enlightener and his son St. Aristaces I as third in line in the-then hereditary Parthian line of catholicoi. He reigned from 333 to 341 AD.

Source (edited): "http://en.wikipedia.org/wiki/St._Vrtanes_I"

Vazgen I

His Holiness **Vazgen I** (also **Vasken I**, Armenian: Վազգեն Ա., born **Levon Garabed Baljian**; September 20, 1908—August 18, 1994) was the Catholicos of the Armenian Apostolic Church between 1955 and 1994, in one of the longest reigns of the Armenian Catholicoi. A native of Romania, he began his career as a philosopher, before becoming a Doctor of Theology and a member of the local Armenian clergy. The leader of the Armenian Apostolic Church hierarchy in Romania, he became Catholicos during the 1950s, moving to the Soviet Union and residing in the Armenian SSR. Vazgen I led the Armenian Church during the dissolution of the Soviet Union, and was the first Catholicos in newly-independent Armenia.

Biography

Vazgen was born in Bucharest to a family belonging to the Armenian-Romanian community. His father was a shoemaker and his mother was a schoolteacher. The young Levon Baljian did not initially pursue the Church as a profession, instead graduating from the University of Bucharest's Faculty of Philosophy and Letters. After graduation, he became a philosopher and published a series of scholarly articles.

As his interests began to shift from philosophy to theology, Baljian studied Armenian Apostolic Theology and Divinity in Athens, Greece. He eventually gained the title of *vardapet*, an ecclesiastical rank for learned preachers and teachers in the Armenian Apostolic Church roughly equivalent to receiving a doctorate in theology. In the 1940s, he became a bishop, and then the *arajnord* (leader) of the Armenian Apostolic Church in Romania.

His rise through the hierarchy of the Church culminated in 1955 when he was elected Catholicos, becoming one of the youngest Catholicoi in the history of the Armenian Apostolic Church. He would reign until his death in 1994. During his long time as Catholicos, he managed to assert some independence for his church in face of the totalitarian Soviet rule in the Armenian SSR, and lived to see religious freedom restored under Armenia's national government in 1991.

From then on, he was very busy renewing ancient Armenian churches and reviving institutions of the church. He saved a number of church treasures by establishing the Alex Manoogian Museum of the Mother Church. Vazgen intensified contacts with the Armenian

Catholic Church, with the aim of reuniting both wings of Armenian Christianity.

Tombstone of Vazgen I near the Mother Cathedral of Holy Etchmiadzin. "Love always perseveres" (Armenian: Սէր ոչ երբէք անկանի) *1 Corinthians 13:7.*

He died on August 18 in 1994, after suffering from a long-term illness.

Source (edited): "http://en.wikipedia.org/wiki/Vazgen_I"

Yeghishe I

Yeghishe I also known as **Yeghishe I Rshtunetsi** (Armenian: Եղիշէ Ա. Ռշտունեցի) (birthday unknown, born in Rshtunik, Armenia – d. 946, Aghtamar, Armenia) was the Catholicos of All Armenians in 941 – 946. Yeghishe I succeeded his brother Catholicos Theodore I. Ruled the Church from Aghtamar, at the time – the Holy See of the Armenian Apostolic Church. Yeghishe Rshtunetsi was the Bishop of Rshtunik and after the death of Theodore I was elected Catholicos by the initiative of the King of Vaspurakan.

Source (edited): "http://en.wikipedia.org/wiki/Yeghishe_I"

Zacharias I of Armenia

Catholicos Zacharias I of Armenia was the Catholicos of the Armenian Apostolic Church between 855 and 876. During his reign a severe earthquake rocked Dvin, during which Zacharias offered powerful prayers. It is said his prayers protected Dvin's church from damage. He died in the twenty-second year of his rule and was buried in Dvin's "cemetery of the holy fathers".

Source (edited): "http://en.wikipedia.org/wiki/Zacharias_I_of_Armenia"

Zaven I

Zaven I (Armenian: Զավեն Ա. Մանազկերտցի) was a catholicos of the Armenian Apostolic Church. He reigned from 377 to 381 AD and second of three catholicoi from the Albaniosid Dynasty.

Source (edited): "http://en.wikipedia.org/wiki/Zaven_I"